BE THERE THEN

A Guide to Exploring Greater Boston's Historic House Museums

Elizabeth S. Levy Merrick

ISBN: 978-1-4834-1921-3 (sc)
ISBN: 978-1-4834-1923-7 (hc)
ISBN: 978-1-4834-1922-0 (e)

Library of Congress Control Number: 2014917769

Because of the dynamic nature of the Internet, any web addresses or links contained in this book may have changed since publication and may no longer be valid. The views expressed in this work are solely those of the author and do not necessarily reflect the views of the publisher, and the publisher hereby disclaims any responsibility for them.

Cover photo: Shirley-Eustis House, Roxbury (Boston), Massachusetts.

Lulu Publishing Services rev. date: 12/01/2014

To the memory of my parents, who loved old houses and the stories they have to tell, and the memory of my aunt Ann, who encouraged me in this endeavor.

And to my husband, who shares my fascination with history, accompanied me enthusiastically on this journey of discovery, and contributed in so many ways to the creation of this book.

CONTENTS

INTRODUCTION

This book is a guide to Boston-area historic house museums—old houses that are open to the public and operated as museums. One of the pleasures of visiting or living in a place such as Boston, with its wealth of historical resources, is to be able to experience the past through the historic houses left to us by earlier residents. Being in the actual buildings where previous lives and dramas played out is quite different from learning about history solely from books, lectures, or online. Valuable as those activities are, the experience of truly being there makes history come alive in a special way.

Many of the house museums highlighted in this book are lesser-known treasures, while others are among the most famous sites in Greater Boston. Whether you are interested in the colonial era, the American Revolution, Victorian times, or anything in between, you will find many choices. Similarly, these houses will reward people with interests ranging from architecture to art to history, or who simply enjoy exploring fascinating places and neighborhoods. Every one of these houses is worth a visit. This guide will help you to choose and prioritize—whether you are a tourist in Boston for a week or a local resident on the lookout for interesting things to do.

How were the houses chosen? This book does not aim to capture every house museum in the Boston area but rather to present a large and varied selection of them. Seeking the truly old, I used the admittedly arbitrary cutoff date of 1900. All of the houses included in this book are within easy reach of Boston by car and/or public transportation. There is a tilt toward the western suburbs in order to include many historic houses in Lexington and Concord.

The guide aims to convey not only the basics of each house but also the overall visitor experience. This is filtered through the lens of my own experience in visiting and researching each of these houses, resulting in a "portrait" of each house. And although this guidebook supplies logistical information, such as admission fees and visiting hours, you should check the museum website or call before visiting since these can and do change. While not noted in each instance, house museums are often closed on holidays.

A note about historic preservation: None of these houses would still exist and be open to the public except for the foresight, generosity, and hard work of donors, community members, and historic preservation organizations. Many of the houses came close to being lost to the wrecking ball. Today we still face choices regarding preservation—and often encounter an uphill battle despite increasing awareness of the value of our historic sites. I urge you to support not only existing house museums but also efforts to protect additional important artifacts of our collective past. These battles to save what is left continue to occur in communities all across the country.

It is my hope that this book will inspire you to visit many of these historic houses, which speak to us of the people and times that helped to shape our own world. So I invite you to turn the page and discover your own favorite portals to the past.

Historic House Locator

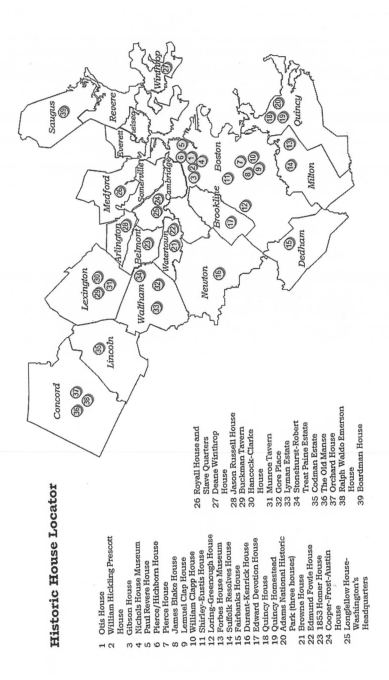

1 Otis House
2 William Hickling Prescott House
3 Gibson House
4 Nichols House Museum
5 Paul Revere House
6 Pierce/Hichborn House
7 Pierce House
8 James Blake House
9 Lemuel Clap House
10 William Clapp House
11 Shirley-Eustis House
12 Loring-Greenough House
13 Forbes House Museum
14 Suffolk Resolves House
15 Fairbanks House
16 Durant-Kenrick House
17 Edward Devotion House
18 Quincy House
19 Quincy Homestead
20 Adams National Historic Park (three houses)
21 Browne House
22 Edmund Fowle House
23 1853 Homer House
24 Cooper-Frost-Austin House
25 Longfellow House-Washington's Headquarters
26 Royall House and Slave Quarters
27 Deane Winthrop House
28 Jason Russell House
29 Buckman Tavern
30 Hancock-Clarke House
31 Munroe Tavern
32 Gore Place
33 Lyman Estate
34 Stonehurst-Robert Treat Paine Estate
35 Codman Estate
36 The Old Manse
37 Orchard House
38 Ralph Waldo Emerson House
39 Boardman House

ADAMS NATIONAL HISTORICAL PARK

Quincy, Massachusetts

Year Built: 1681 (John Adams Birthplace); c. 1716 (John Quincy Adams Birthplace); 1731 (Old House at Peacefield)

What's Special: *Birthplaces of Presidents John Adams and John Quincy Adams; three historic houses within the park; historic library building; lovely gardens*

The Adams National Historical Park is a place that warrants spending half a day to take everything in. Start at the visitor center, where you purchase tickets and await the trolley that will take you on your sightseeing journey. Visitors are scheduled for tours every thirty minutes on a first-come, first-served basis. It can get very busy here so sometimes you may have a wait. That will give you time to watch the excellent introductory film, which features Laura Linney and Paul Giamatti portraying President John Adams and his remarkable wife, Abigail (as in the acclaimed PBS special).

The park has a stellar trio of historic houses connected with the famous presidential families of founding father John Adams and his son, John Quincy Adams. The two birthplaces are saltbox-style dwellings that stand next to each other. The John Adams Birthplace dates to 1681. John Adams's father was a farmer and cobbler. The house is furnished with reproductions appropriate to the period and includes a room set up with shoemaking materials. The birthplace of John Quincy Adams was given to John and Abigail Adams as a wedding present in 1764. It is larger and has more decorative features than the earlier home.

After guided tours of these houses, the trolley will take you to Peacefield, the property where four generations of the Adams family lived up until 1927. The original part of the "Old House" at Peacefield was built in 1731 as a summer house for the Vassal family, who were prominent in colonial life. Enlarged by later additions, Peacefield is gracious and welcoming rather than imposing. The furnishings belonged to the Adams family, spanning all four generations. A special room is the study where John Adams died on July 4, 1826—exactly fifty years after the adoption of the Declaration of Independence. He died on the same day as Thomas Jefferson, his long-time colleague and friend with whom he reconciled late in life after they had become painfully estranged. Next to Peacefield is the picturesque Stone Library, built in 1870 after John Quincy Adams's death, in accordance with his will, to accommodate his books and documents.

Also at Peacefield are orchards and formal gardens that blaze with bright blooms in season. The gardens include original plantings of roses, lilac, and boxwood that thrive to this day, as well as more recently planted flowers. On a pleasant day, meandering through the gardens is a wonderful way to conclude your visit before getting back on the trolley. If you want to extend your visit further, you can take a short walk from the visitor center to the United First Parish Church, where both presidents and their wives are buried.

To Visit

Location: Visitor center at 1250 Hancock Street, Quincy, MA 02169

Opening hours: Visitor center and all houses open mid-April through mid-November, daily, 9:00 a.m.–5:00 p.m. From mid-November until mid-April, the visitor center is open Tuesday through Friday, 10:00 a.m.–4:00 p.m., but the historic houses are not open.

Type of tour: Guided.

Admission fees: $5/person, children under sixteen free. Free admission with "America the Beautiful" National Park Service pass. (Note: these passes are an amazing bargain.)

Elizabeth S. Levy Merrick

Directions by car: From Boston, take I-93 South to exit 7 for Route 3 South to Braintree and Cape Cod. Take the first exit off Route 3 South (exit 19) and follow signs toward Quincy Center. Continue straight on Burgin Parkway through six sets of traffic lights. At the seventh set of traffic lights, turn right onto Dimmock Street. Follow Dimmock Street one block to the intersection of Hancock Street. Turn right onto Hancock Street. The National Park Service Visitor Center, located in the Galleria at President's Place, is two blocks on your left.

Parking: There is free validated parking in the Galleria garage in the rear of the visitor center building; turn left on Saville Avenue just before the building.

Directions by public transportation: From Boston, take the MBTA Red Line to Quincy Center Station. Turn right upon exiting the train, and at the top of the stairs, turn left and exit the station to Hancock Street. Walk across Hancock Street to the visitor center.

More information: This property is owned by the National Park Service. Website: www.nps.gov Phone: 617-770-1175

Elizabeth S. Levy Merrick

BOARDMAN HOUSE

Saugus, Massachusetts

Year Built: 1692

What's Special: Seventeenth-century house with largely original structure and details

Marooned amid encroaching bungalows and ranches, facing a busy street, the Boardman House is an ancient survivor. Originally the home of William Boardman, a seventeenth-century joiner, and his large family, it was previously surrounded by a three hundred–acre farm. Generations of Boardman descendants lived here and changed relatively few features of the house. Fortunately, when the last heir sold the house to a developer, the early preservationist William Sumner Appleton purchased it for posterity.

The front of the house has the slightly overhanging second floor reminiscent of medieval Europe (and common in First Period houses—those built in the colonies during the seventeenth century). However, gables were removed at some point. The house is unfurnished, and thus the focus of visiting here is the architecture and interior woodwork, including some decorative flourishes that William Boardman might have crafted himself. Visitors can see and learn about the bare bones of the house—how it was constructed and fortunately preserved. The house has a remarkable amount of original building material still intact, including oak clapboards.

An interesting story shared on the tour is that the Boardman House was known for many years as the Scotch House, referring to the structure in which a number of Scottish prisoners from the English Civil War were housed. In the 1650s, a house in this locale was built for these prisoners who were sold into indentured servitude; for many years, it was believed that Boardman House and Scotch House were one and the same. It is now known that Boardman House is not the Scotch House, which is no longer standing—a local historical mystery solved.

To Visit

Location: 17 Howard Street, Saugus, MA 01906

Opening hours: June 1–October 15, first Saturday of the month, 11:00 a.m.–3:00 p.m.

Type of tour: Guided.

Admission fees: $5/adults, $4/seniors, $2.50/students. Free for Historic New England members and Saugus residents.

Directions by car: From Boston, take Route 1 North to Saugus and take the exit marked "Main Street, Wakefield." Follow Main Street northwest for about three-quarters of a mile, then turn left just past the Village Park Shopping Center onto Howard Street. Boardman House is on the right.

Parking: There is a small area designated for parking next to the house, and street parking is also allowed.

Directions by public transportation: Boardman House is difficult to reach from Boston by public transportation. From downtown Boston, take the MBTA Orange Line—Oak Grove to Malden Station. Then get the #430 bus toward Saugus Center. Get off at Main Street and Pierce Memorial Drive. Boardman House is a twenty-minute walk from there.

More information: This property is owned by Historic New England. Website: www.historicnewengland.org Phone: 978-768-3632

BROWNE HOUSE

Watertown, Massachusetts

Year Built: 1698

What's Special: Original First Period (seventeenth-century American colonial) house; early example of restoration based on modern principles; off the beaten track

Browne House is completely hidden from view as the busy stream of traffic passes by. In fact, it is easy to miss even when you are looking for it. (Turn into the police station parking lot next door.) Behind its overgrown hedges, this house built in 1698 seems to nestle in a time capsule on its remaining spot of land.

This is the second house to stand on this lot; the first one burned. The 1698 structure, which remains, was added to in 1720. There is a remaining peaked gable with a medieval-style overhang. Only the 1698 portion, comprised of three rooms, is open to the public.

Browne House has served at different points as a family home, inn, and tea room. For decades the house was owned by the Brownes, a prominent family in Watertown. In the early twentieth century, it was saved by the early preservationist William Sumner Appleton, who rescued the house, even though it was in a sad state of deterioration. He did so despite the naysayers who thought it was not worthwhile. The restoration that ensued was one of the first to follow a scientific approach to historical accuracy based on evidence rather than current taste or a sentimentalized version of the past.

Elizabeth S. Levy Merrick

On the first floor, the only room open is the dark, low-ceilinged lower chamber with the original great hearth and diamond-pattern, leaded-pane windows. This room was a multipurpose one, providing space for cooking, eating, sitting, and sleeping for some of the family members. This room is highly atmospheric and will take you back to early New England days. The upper chamber above, a bedroom that also accommodated inn guests, has special features, such as a rare style of mantelpiece and original door hinges. There is also a display of photographs and text regarding the restoration process. The attic would have provided more sleeping quarters in the days of the Browne family. The house contains many period furnishings, both from the Browne family and elsewhere.

Browne House is typically open only a few days a year, but if you are a seventeenth-century house enthusiast, a visit to the Browne House warrants planning ahead for.

To Visit

Location: 562 Main Street, Watertown, MA 02472

Opening hours: Typically open to the public four days per year between April and October. Check website in the spring for upcoming season dates. Tours on the hour 11:00 a.m.–4:00 p.m., last tour at 4:00 p.m.

Type of tour: Guided.

Admission fees: $5/adults, $4/seniors, $2.50/students. Free for Historic New England members and Watertown residents.

Directions by car: From downtown Boston, take Storrow Drive west, continue on Soldiers Field Road, and then bear right, following signs for US-20 West/North Beacon Street/Leo M. Birmingham Parkway as you travel over the North Beacon Street Bridge. Follow North Beacon Street into Watertown Square. Then follow Main Street (Route 20) west to the house.

Parking: Park in the police station parking lot next door to the house.

Directions by public transportation: Several routes are available. One is to take the MBTA Red Line to Central Square (Cambridge). Then take the #70 Cedarwood bus. The place to catch this bus is at the intersection of Green and Magazine Streets in Cambridge.

More information: This property is owned by Historic New England. Website: www.historicnewengland.org Phone: 617-994-6660

Elizabeth S. Levy Merrick

BUCKMAN TAVERN

Lexington, Massachusetts

Year Built: 1710

What's Special: *Major American Revolution site; evocative and authentic restoration; excellent self-paced audiotour; interesting gallery exhibit*

Lexington is a treasure trove for history buffs, and Buckman Tavern is one of its gems. Anyone interested in the American Revolution will be thrilled by a visit here. The tavern was owned by John Buckman, a patriot, and run by himself, his family, and servants. It hosted many town meetings, including some at which the topic was arming the militia. The tavern is located on the town green in Lexington, where the outnumbered local militia bravely stood with their muskets awaiting the arrival of the British regulars as they advanced on April 19, 1775. The militia first gathered at this centrally located tavern. It is electrifying to stand at the front window today and imagine how militia members and their families felt in the tense hours leading up to the arrival of the redcoats.

The details of what happened on Battle Green that day—who shot first and indeed to what extent the militia members shot at the British troops at all—have been hotly contested and remain unclear. There are reports that the first shot was actually fired from the tavern. Some have claimed that the confrontation at Lexington, which left eight militia members dead, was simply a massacre and that the first true battle happened later at Concord. But there is no dispute over whether the events at Lexington galvanized the patriots that day and helped set off the war.

The tavern is also fascinating simply as a place to immerse yourself in the life of the period. The perfectly restored tavern includes the taproom where men would drink and discuss politics as well as the more genteel parlor where ladies would take tea—the herbal sort, once the boycott of tea had begun. In the kitchen with its huge hearth, visitors observe all of the period utensils and equipment needed to produce food for the household and paying guests. Buckman Tavern is highly evocative, particularly since the rooms are set up precisely as they would have been in the eighteenth century: tables set for tea, mugs ready to be refilled in the taproom.

Rather than offering guided tours, Buckman Tavern has recently produced a superb self-paced audio tour. It provides just the right amount of information about life at the tavern, and in Lexington more broadly, on the eve of the revolution. This enables visitors to place what they see in the context of social customs and political currents at a key time in the nation's history. The audio tour is enhanced by music and narrative, including the words of those long departed.

After your tour of the historically accurate rooms, visit the gallery space upstairs. There is an exhibit addressing the controversy as to whether Lexington or Concord is the town that deserves credit for where the war actually started. You can hear the conflicting testimony that has fueled the debate and then vote on where you think it started.

To Visit

Location: 1 Bedford Street, Lexington, MA 02420

Opening hours: Daily, April–October; 10:00 a.m.–4:00 p.m.

Type of tour: Self-guided audio tour.

Admission fees: $7/adult, $5/child (ages six to sixteen). Children under six are free. Note that combined admission to three Lexington historic houses (Buckman Tavern, Munroe Tavern, and the Hancock-Clarke House) may be purchased for $12/adult, $8/child.

Directions by car: From Boston, take I-93 North to exit 37B to merge onto I-95/128 South toward Waltham. Take exit 31A to merge onto MA-225 East/

MA-4 South/Bedford Street toward Lexington. Buckman Tavern is about 1.6 miles, on Bedford Street at Lexington's Battle Green.

Parking: Street parking is available.

Directions by public transportation: From Boston and Cambridge (Monday–Saturday) take the MBTA Red Line to Alewife Station. Bus routes #76 (Hanscom Air Force Base) and #62 (Bedford VA Hospital) run to and from Alewife Station. Get off at Lexington Center.

More information: This property is owned by the Lexington Historical Society. Website: www.lexingtonhistory.org Phone: 781-862-5598

CODMAN ESTATE

Lincoln, Massachusetts

Year Built: c. 1740

What's Special: *Impressive Federal-style mansion; lavishly furnished with Codman family possessions; extensive land and gardens*

Unlike many of the great historic houses, the Codman Estate, or "The Grange," remains an estate to this day: a grand country house surrounded by extensive lawns, gardens, and woods. Part of the pleasure in visiting this property is the drive along the way. If you come from Route 2, you will drive down a country road, past Thoreau's Walden Pond and on into Lincoln, with fields and woods stretching away on either side. Lincoln is one of the greenest and most beautiful Boston suburbs, thanks to its extensive conservation land. Turn into the Codman Estate drive, and the sight of this three-story Federal mansion in its bucolic setting may convey the same sense of welcome that the Codmans undoubtedly experienced when they would arrive at their summer home each season.

The first owner of the house was Chambers Russell, a prominent citizen and founder of the town of Lincoln, who also maintained a farm there. Subsequently several generations of the prominent Codman family—who made a fortune in shipping and trade—owned and enlarged the original house into the impressive Federal-style mansion it is now. A later Codman owner was Ogden Codman, a renowned architect and interior designer. This "house on a hill" presides over a wide sweep of lawn, a pond, and

Elizabeth S. Levy Merrick

gardens, including a hidden Italian garden complete with a lily pad–festooned reflecting pool.

This is a mansion worthy of the term and has been restored to perfect condition. Your first step through the front door into the entry hall will reveal a marvelously ornate staircase with arches over its various flights. The dining room is an unusual Victorian-era treasure with butternut woodwork patterns on the ceiling, a Samurai-shield chandelier, and magnificent fireplace and mantel complete with carved lions. Another special room is the elegant hall, or ballroom, with French windows on two sides that open onto the grounds. The house is filled with the family's furniture and art, much of it European. There are other interesting reflections of different time periods, including a late nineteenth-century bathroom and a pantry with a massive 1885 coal stove manufactured in Boston.

Although the third floor is closed to the public, there is an abundance of rooms to view. You will enjoy a very full visit at this large, elegant house, which looks as if the Codman family could walk in any moment and be pleased that all is in order. Save time to see the gardens and perhaps to explore the nature trails on adjoining conservation lands. You will want to linger.

To Visit

Location: 34 Codman Road, Lincoln, MA 01773

Opening hours: June 1–October 15. Second and fourth Saturdays of the month, 11:00 a.m.–5:00 p.m. Tours on the hour, last tour at 4:00 p.m.

Type of tour: Guided.

Admission fees: $5/adults, $4/seniors, $2.50/students. Free for Historic New England members and Lincoln residents.

Directions by car: From Boston, take I-90 Mass Pike West to exit 15 (Route 128/I-95 North) toward Waltham. From Route 128, take exit 26 (US 20/Waltham/Weston). Take US 20 East toward Waltham, and take a quick, sharp left onto Stow Street. After 0.2 miles, take a left onto Route 117 West/Main Street. Go about four miles and take a slight right onto Codman Road. An alternate route from the Boston/Cambridge area is to take Route 2 West to Route 126 East past Walden Pond. Take third left on Codman Road. Codman Estate is 0.5 miles on the left.

Parking: Parking lot on the grounds adjacent to main gate.

Directions by public transportation: From downtown Boston, take MBTA Green Line to North Station. Take the Fitchburg or South Acton commuter rail from North Station and get off at Lincoln Station. Walk southwest down Lincoln Road to Codman Road. The Codman Estate is about half a mile from the station.

More information: This property is owned by Historic New England. Website: www.historicnewengland.org Phone: 617-994-6690.

Elizabeth S. Levy Merrick

COOPER-FROST-AUSTIN HOUSE

Cambridge, Massachusetts

Year Built: 1681

What's Special: *Oldest dwelling still standing in Cambridge; architecturally significant features; very atmospheric*

The Cooper-Frost-Austin House used to sit at the edge of the Cambridge Common back when the common provided communal grazing land. Now the common is smaller and the house is located in a dense but charming Cambridge neighborhood. This is the oldest house still standing in the city of Cambridge. Happily, it looks and feels as old as it really is. Those in search of atmosphere will find it here.

The earliest part of the house was built in 1681 by Samuel Cooper, a church deacon and town selectman. The sloping saltbox silhouette remains, with its one-story lean-to section coming close to the ground in the back. This is one of the oldest "integral lean-to" houses (in which the house and lean-to were built as one structure rather than adding on the lean-to) in New England. There is a seventeenth-century side gable overhanging as well. The gables in front are long gone, however, with Georgian- and Federal-period additions. The house stayed in the same extended family for 250 years. During that time, there were major changes to the house, including a 1720 addition that provides for a much larger house and symmetrical appearance.

The real treat is inside, however. The warren of low-ceilinged rooms around the central chimney seems securely anchored in the distant past. This is true despite some modern-day furnishings due to the fact the house is occupied by a caretaker. A host of nooks and crannies, special features such as the huge seventeenth-century hearth in what was originally the hall, and what is possibly the oldest arched door in North America make touring this house an adventure.

This is not one of those perfectly restored and thoroughly polished house museums; rather, you will see and appreciate many imperfections that speak of age. There is plenty to study here for the architecture aficionado, but simply absorbing the sights and feel of this ancient house will be a rare opportunity for many visitors. Some areas are a mix of time periods. Watch your head as you step into what is now a working kitchen (originally a bedroom) with a low ceiling, wide, bumpy floor planks, and a 1930s-era sink.

The grounds are modest, but there is a bit of pleasant green space. You may contemplate what the house and neighborhood might have looked like back in 1681, and consider how fortunate we are that Samuel Cooper's house still stands as a reminder of our colonial heritage.

To Visit

Location: 21 Linnaean St., Cambridge, MA 02138

Opening hours: Typically open to the public several days per year, April–August. Tours at noon, 1:30 p.m., and 3:00 p.m. Check the website for current season openings.

Type of tour: Guided.

Admission fees: $5/ adults, $4/seniors, $2.50/students, free for Historic New England members and Cambridge residents.

Directions by car: From downtown Boston, follow Massachusetts Avenue across the river to Harvard Square and continue west on Massachusetts Avenue toward Arlington. Several blocks after passing Cambridge Common, take a left on Linnaean Street. House is on the right.

Parking: There is some street parking available for nonresidents on Linnaean Street. Otherwise, there is metered parking on Massachusetts Avenue.

Directions by public transportation: Take the MBTA Red Line to Harvard Square or Porter Square. Linnaean Street is a fairly short walk down Massachusetts Avenue from either station.

More information: This property is owned by Historic New England. Website: www.historicnewengland.org Phone: 617-994-6669

DEANE WINTHROP HOUSE

Winthrop, Massachusetts

Year Built: 1637

What's Special: *Reportedly the oldest continually occupied, wood-framed home in the country; prominent colonial family; off the beaten track*

The Deane Winthrop House is a hardy antique, very incongruous in its current neighborhood filled with pleasant homes of recent vintage. The oldest part of the house was built by Captain William Pierce, a privateer, in 1637. At that time, the house fronted the ocean, which is now more distant due to landfill. Governor John Winthrop purchased the house after the captain's death on the Spanish Main. It was a wedding present for his second son, Deane Winthrop. Various wings of the house were added later in the seventeenth century. Members of the Winthrop family remained in the house until early in the eighteenth century, when a succession of other owners held the title.

This house is said to be the oldest continually occupied, wood-framed dwelling in the United States. Currently it is occupied by caretakers who provide tours by appointment. Thus, the tours have a very personal feel and are conducted in what is contemporary living space.

This is a fascinating house, with many rooms to explore. It contains a mix of antiques (some from the Winthrop family) and modern furnishings. The furnishings and artifacts span the life of the house, ranging from a Revolutionary War cannonball (this area was a lookout surveying Boston Harbor) to an 1850s sewing machine. And every room and item has stories

Elizabeth S. Levy Merrick

that your guides will be happy to share, not least of which is a close-to-firsthand report of Captain Pierce's ghost in one of the bedrooms.

This house has survived through so many different eras, some largely forgotten but which you can learn about on your visit. For example, it is a little-known fact that during the late 1800s, Winthrop was a summer destination for Bostonians seeking a break from the city.

You will find the Deane Winthrop House an interesting experience. You can also congratulate yourself for getting so far off the beaten path—while venturing only a few miles outside of Boston.

To Visit

Location: 40 Shirley Street, Winthrop, MA 02152

Opening hours: By appointment.

Type of tour: Guided.

Admission fees: $5 donation is requested.

Directions by car: From Boston, take the Callahan Tunnel toward Logan Airport. Continue to follow signs for Route 1A North for 1.9 miles. Keep left at the fork, follow signs for 1A North/Revere, and merge onto 1A North. Go 1.5 miles, then turn right onto Boardman Street. At the rotary, take second exit onto Saratoga Street. Continue onto Main Street, and continue onto Revere Street. Take right onto Shirley Street.

Parking: Street parking is available.

Directions by public transportation: It is not easy to get here by public transportation. If you choose to, you can take the MBTA Blue Line toward Wonderland and get off at Beachmont Station. From Beachmont Station and Winthrop Avenue, board the #119 bus and get off at Crescent Avenue and Winthrop Parkway. The house is about a twenty-minute walk from there. Walk right onto Winthrop Avenue (the parkway goes to the left), stay on it as it becomes Revere Street, and follow that until you take a left onto Shirley Street.

More information: This property is owned by the Winthrop Improvement and Historical Association. Website: None currently. Phone: 617- 846-8606.

Elizabeth S. Levy Merrick

DURANT-KENRICK HOUSE

Newton, Massachusetts

Year Built: c. 1734

What's Special: *Unique, interactive museum; perfect for children; narratives of three prominent local families who lived in the house; pleasant grounds*

The Durant-Kenrick House is one of a kind. The way this Georgian farmhouse has been interpreted as a museum provides an exciting way to introduce anyone—but especially children—to colonial life and later American history. Through its self-guided tour, the house provides a window into various themes of American history, including the revolution and slavery, by relating the narratives of three families that successively inhabited the Durant-Kenrick House. The Durants were a prominent eighteenth-century Newton family, large landowners and merchants. The Kenricks arrived later and established a commercial nursery noted among horticulturalists. Finally, the Dewings lived here during the twentieth century and helped to ensure that the house would eventually become a museum.

Each room of the house is divided into two sections: the historic section, with period furniture and a standing, cut-out silhouette of someone who lived in the house, and the modern section with interactive games and materials to enhance the experience for children. The games and activities are hands-on and engaging—buttons to press, materials to touch, and problems to solve, such as how to utilize a ninety-one-acre farm in a way that will best support your family.

The Durant-Kenrick House is a large, well-crafted, and expensively furnished home, reflecting the status of the prominent and accomplished families who lived here. It is located in an attractive residential neighborhood of stately homes. The Durant-Kenrick House is the one painted a rich green, a rarely seen but historically accurate color.

It is a rather magical experience to walk through the house, since in some rooms your footstep will set off audio recordings that truly bring history to life. For example, in the Durant parlor, you will hear political discourse in the wake of the Boston Tea Party while refreshments (certainly not including real tea) are served. Or you may see the interior of a picture frame come alive with portrayals of an abolitionist Kenrick family member's experience of Southern slave culture.

This house museum opened recently, so many history lovers have not yet discovered it. A trip here is richly rewarding and thoroughly fun for visitors of all ages. It is a glowing example of how to make history come alive in a creative way without succumbing to the lure of computer monitors and high-tech approaches, which can paradoxically detract from the very experience they are meant to enhance.

In addition, there is some lovely green space around the house, with a lawn and mature trees. The gardens are being planted with flowers and fruit trees that were all featured in the Kenrick Nurseries' horticultural catalog.

To Visit

Location: 286 Waverley Avenue, Newton, MA 02458

Opening hours: Year-round, Wednesday–Friday, 12:00–4:00 p.m., Saturday and Sunday, 10:00 a.m.–4:00 p.m. Closed on major holidays.

Type of tour: Self-guided.

Admission fees: $6/adults; $5/children, seniors, Newton residents; free to members of Historic Newton.

Elizabeth S. Levy Merrick

Directions by car: From Boston, take I-90/Massachusetts Turnpike West to exit 17 to Washington Street, following the signs for West Newton. Turn left on Church Street and follow it over the Massachusetts Turnpike and up the hill to where Church Street ends, about 0.7 miles. Turn right onto Waverley Avenue. The house is on the left, just past the traffic light.

Parking: Limited parking in lot and plenty of on-street parking on the even-numbered side of Waverley Avenue and Kenrick Street.

Directions by public transportation: Numerous bus routes stop within a short walk of the house, including #52, 57, 504, 553, 556, and 558. From downtown Boston, one option is to take MBTA Green Line to Kenmore Station, then take bus #57 Watertown Yard via Brighton. Get off at Tremont Street and Playstead Road. It is somewhat more than a half-mile walk to the house.

More information: This property is owned by Historic Newton. Website: www.newtonma.gov/gov/historic Phone: 617-641-9142

Edmund Fowle House

Watertown, Massachusetts

Year Built: 1772

What's Special: *Significant as a seat of Revolutionary War government; restored to 1775 appearance*

This is a handsomely restored house with a very proud history. The Edmund Fowle House's main claim to fame is that the executive council of the Massachusetts Legislature met here regularly from 1775 to 1776 to conduct the work of governing Massachusetts during that early phase of the revolution. The council included some of the most famous patriot leaders, such as John Adams, Samuel Adams, and John Hancock, who came to Watertown when not required at the Continental Congress in Philadelphia. When, in July 1776, a copy of the Declaration of Independence arrived in Watertown, it was read to the public from the window of the Council Chamber. Also, the first international treaty (with two Native American tribes) engaged in by the United States was signed here.

At the top of the small, winding staircase, the L-shaped Council Chamber on the second floor has been restored to its earlier appearance. Other rooms of the house, which was owned by a farmer and merchant Edmund Fowle but requisitioned when war broke out, are also of interest. The "best room" or parlor has been painted in its original gold and contains a copy of the John Singleton Copley portrait of Dr. Joseph Warren, president of the Provincial Congress in 1775 who was killed at the Battle of Bunker Hill.

Elizabeth S. Levy Merrick

The Watertown Historical Society has owned the Edmund Fowle House since 1922 and is still headquartered there. So it makes sense that some rooms have been adapted for current uses and that various artifacts, such as a doll cradle made of splintered wood from a Boston Tea Party tea chest, can be found there. On one visit, there was also an exhibition of work by a local nineteenth-century painter, Ellen Robbins.

If you are visiting in July, check ahead to see when the annual reenactment of the reading of the Declaration of Independence will take place—or just picture the crowd outside in 1776 hearing those fateful words for the first time.

To Visit

Location: 28 Marshall Street, Watertown, MA 02472

Opening hours: Year-round, third Sunday of each month from 1:00 p.m. till 4:00 p.m. or by appointment. The last scheduled tour begins at 3:15 p.m.

Type of tour: Guided.

Admission fees: $5/adults, $3/under twelve and over sixty-five.

Directions by car: From Boston, take Storrow Drive West, continue on Soldiers Field Road, and then continue on North Beacon Street. Take a right onto Mount Auburn Street, then after about one-third of a mile make a left on Marshall Street. House is on left.

Parking: There is plenty of street parking.

Directions by public transportation: Take the MBTA Red Line to Harvard Station. At Harvard Station, take the #71 Watertown Square via Mount Auburn Street bus to Marshall Street and Mount Auburn Street. The house is a few minutes' walk from there.

More information: This property is owned by the Watertown Historical Society. Website: www.historicalsocietyofwatertownma.org Phone: 617-923-6067

Elizabeth S. Levy Merrick

EDWARD DEVOTION HOUSE

Brookline, Massachusetts

Year Built: c. 1740

What's Special: *Rare eighteenth-century house in this location; interesting view of local history*

It is not all that often that you find a colonial-era house museum just a stone's throw from a landmark bagel shop known throughout the region as among the best ... but the Edward Devotion House is one such. This illustrates the changes in the neighborhood as life went on around the mid-eighteenth-century Edward Devotion House.

The Edward Devotion House is both a house museum and the headquarters for the Brookline Historical Society. The current structure dates to about 1740 but incorporates the house frame of an earlier dwelling from the seventeenth century. Edward Devotion Sr. owned substantial farmland in what was then called Muddy River. Muddy River was an agricultural community that was originally part of Boston and only later became the independent town of Brookline.

The house is a solid building of modest size, somewhat unassuming from the outside. It is surrounded on several sides by buildings of the Edward Devotion School, which resulted from the bequest of Edward Devotion Jr. for public education purposes. It is also adjacent to a park that provides a nice buffer from busy Harvard Street.

Inside, there are some ornate moldings and a carved staircase that reflect a desire for more than a merely utilitarian house. Three rooms are open to the public, including the parlor, all filled with eighteenth- and nineteenth-century furnishings as well as artifacts related to the history of Brookline.

The rarity of this vintage of house in the area, along with the mélange of period rooms and local history information, make for an interesting visit at the Edward Devotion House. And as hinted at earlier, its location in the thriving Coolidge Corner section of Brookline means you can easily combine your visit with a snack from Kupel's (the landmark bagel mecca) or one of the many other shops lining Harvard Street. It is also near the John F. Kennedy birthplace, a National Historical Site in Brookline.

To Visit

Location: 347 Harvard Street, Brookline, MA 02446

Opening hours: June-October, first and third Sundays of the month, 12:00-3:00 p.m.

Type of tour: Guided.

Admission fees: Donation requested.

Directions by car: From Boston, drive west (away from downtown) on Beacon Street until you get to the intersection of Harvard Street in Brookline. Turn right on Harvard Street. The house is a couple of blocks down on the right, though very difficult to see from the street.

Parking: There is street parking and a public parking lot just off Harvard Street.

Directions by public transportation: Take the MBTA Green Line C train toward Cleveland Circle and get off at the Coolidge Corner stop. The house is just a few minutes' walk from there.

More information: This property is owned by the Brookline Historical Society. Website: www.brooklinehistoricalsociety.org Phone: 617-566-5747

1853 HOMER HOUSE

Belmont, Massachusetts

Year Built: 1853

What's Special: *Connection with artist Winslow Homer; elegant Victorian mansion*

This Victorian Italianate mansion, set proudly on a hill in Belmont's Pleasant Street Historic District, belonged to the uncle of famed artist Winslow Homer. Winslow Flagg Homer built this house for his family in 1853, sparing no expense. His nephew spent substantial time here, and some of Winslow Homer's earlier works reflect the house and landscape, including his famous *Croquet Scene* reportedly set on the front lawn.

The house makes a grand impression outside and in. With its tall windows, fourteen-foot ceilings, ornate moldings, marble fireplaces, and carved doors, the house reflects wonderful craftsmanship and elegance. Step through the front door into a large center hall with turquoise-flowered stained glass and a curving suspended staircase. Chandeliers seem to be sparkling everywhere. The dining room is striking due to its oval shape, curved doors and dark, heavy carvings and sideboard.

On the second floor are bedrooms, a parlor with tall Italianate windows, and a charming light-filled sewing room with pocket doors and a tree-top view. The house is filled with period furniture. A small room on this floor is devoted to exhibiting materials and works from Winslow Homer's career as an illustrator for popular magazines.

Elizabeth S. Levy Merrick

The venerable Belmont Woman's Club owns the Homer House. In addition to regularly scheduled tours during the summer, there are special events throughout the year. These have included "Downton Abbey Afternoon" and the annual holiday open house. What better way to get into the holiday spirit than by nibbling on delicious treats and sipping punch as you survey the house with its seasonal decorations?

Note, too, that the location of the Homer House makes for an extra-enjoyable excursion. You can take a leisurely stroll through the lovely Pleasant Street Historic District and browse the shops or have lunch in lively, walkable Belmont Center. Another draw is that although it feels far from urban life, it is very easily accessible by public transportation.

To Visit

Location: 661 Pleasant Street, Belmont, MA 02478

Opening hours: June–August. Tours on Friday at 1:00 p.m., Saturday at 12:00, 1:00, 2:00, and 3:00 p.m.

Type of tour: Guided.

Admission fees: $10/adults, $5/children ages five to twelve. Members free.

Directions by car: From downtown Boston, take Storrow Drive west and continue on to Soldiers Field Road, bearing right on Eliot Bridge to Cambridge, following signs for Route 2/Route 16/Arlington/Fresh Pond Parkway. At the first traffic rotary, take the third exit (making a left turn) to get onto Concord Avenue. At next traffic rotary, go around and continue straight on Concord Avenue into Belmont. In about 1.7 miles, take a right to stay on Concord Avenue, passing under the railway bridge, then take immediate left to continue on Concord Avenue. Take a right on Pleasant Street. House is on the corner.

Parking: Limited street parking on Pleasant Street. Additional parking available in Belmont Center—metered street parking and municipal lot.

Directions by public transportation: Take the MBTA Red Line to Harvard Station. At Harvard Square, buses #74 and #75 go to Belmont Center, where the 1853 Homer House is located. You can also take the MBTA commuter rail (Acton-Fitchburg line) from North Station in Boston or Porter Square in Cambridge to Belmont Center.

More information: This property is owned by the Belmont Woman's Club. Website: www.belmontwomansclub.org Phone: 617-484-4892

Elizabeth S. Levy Merrick

FAIRBANKS HOUSE

Dedham, Massachusetts

Year Built: c. 1637

What's Special: Oldest remaining timber-frame house in North America; sections from many different periods; highly evocative; still owned by descendants of original occupants

Your first glimpse of this house with its plain clapboard exterior and steeply sloping roof will reveal that you have hit the colonial historic-house jackpot. The Fairbanks House has it all for true lovers of very old houses: original architecture, family history and furnishings, and a heavy dose of atmosphere. This house looks and feels ancient. Indeed, in one room, the ceiling sags so low that it is impossible for a tall person to stand up. But in fact, the entire house has been lovingly preserved by Fairbanks descendants right up to the present day.

The Fairbanks family in America originated with Jonathan and Grace Fairbanks, Puritans who came from England and established a prosperous life for their large family. He was a skilled craftsman who built spinning wheels and looms. His former workspace contains examples of these objects. Eight generations of the family lived in the house. When a developer bought the house in the early 1900s with plans to tear it down, descendants bought it back, and it is now owned and opened to the public by the Fairbanks Family in America Association. Family pride is evident. Fairbanks family members include Charles Fairbanks, who was Theodore Roosevelt's vice president and after whom the well-known city in Alaska was named.

Touring the house is a real journey of discovery because while the original portion dates to 1637, many additions were built, and at one point a separate building was even moved and attached as a further addition. So you will travel from Puritan times—witness the hex mark carved over the hearth to ward off witchcraft—to the nineteenth century simply by crossing thresholds. In total, it is a very large house with many rooms to take in. The house is filled with family belongings from every period, donated by descendants, although it is generally not known which may have actually been in the house when the early Fairbanks generations resided here. The belongings include Civil War and Revolutionary War artifacts.

As a visitor, you will feel both warmly welcomed and privileged to share in the heritage of this family, which provides a wonderful window into the broader heritage of America. Indeed, for many reasons, the Fairbanks House is not to be missed.

To Visit

Location: 511 East Street, Dedham, MA 02026

Opening hours: May through October, Tuesday–Saturday 10:00 a.m.–3:00 p.m. and Sunday 1:00–3:00 p.m. Tours begin every hour on the hour, with the last tour beginning at 3:00.

Type of tour: Guided.

Admission fees: $12/adults, $10/seniors and AAA members, $6/children ages six to twelve, children under six free, $35/family rate.

Directions by car: From Boston, there are numerous possible routes. One option is to take I-93 South, continue for about fifteen miles, then continue onto Route 1, and continue to Route 1/I-95 South. Get off at exit 14 toward East Street/Canton Street to Dedham. At the traffic rotary, take the first right onto East Street. After 0.9 miles, at the traffic rotary stay straight to remain on East Street. The Fairbanks House is on the left.

Parking: Street parking available in addition to a small parking lot.

Elizabeth S. Levy Merrick

Directions by public transportation: It is possible though not convenient to reach the Fairbanks House by public transportation. From downtown Boston, take the MBTA Orange Line to Forest Hills Station. Then board the #34E bus for Walpole Center via Dedham Mall, and get off at Dedham Center. It is about a ten- to fifteen-minute walk from there to the Fairbanks House. At the main intersection, turn right onto High Street. Walk about one block and turn right onto Eastern Avenue. Cross Route 1 and continue past the VFW Post and American Legion. The Fairbanks House is on the right.

Alternatively, you can take the MBTA commuter rail Franklin Line train from South Station or Back Bay Station in Boston to Endicott Station in Dedham. It is about a twenty-five-minute walk from the station to the Fairbanks House. Walk down the hill and turn right onto East Street. The Fairbanks House will be on the left. Be sure to check the commuter rail schedule in both directions when planning your trip, as trains are not always frequent.

More information: This property is owned by the Fairbanks Family in America, Inc. Website: www.fairbankshouse.org Phone: 781-326-1170

FORBES HOUSE MUSEUM

Milton, Massachusetts

Year Built: 1833

What's Special: Greek Revival architecture; China trade furnishings; Abraham Lincoln birthplace replica and memorabilia; extensive park-like grounds.

The Forbes House is a nineteenth-century Greek Revival mansion set on Milton Hill, overlooking open fields with a view of Boston Harbor. It was one of numerous country estates in the area at that time. The house was built in 1833 for Margaret Perkins Forbes by her sons, one of whom was Captain Robert Bennet Forbes, a successful China trade merchant. The house is filled with exquisite furniture and decorative arts that Captain Forbes brought back—a very special feature of this historic house museum.

Even if the China trade is not of particular interest to you, the house has great appeal in other ways. It is a gracious and beautifully proportioned building furnished with a mix of both Asian and other period articles. The items belonged to the Forbes family, who lived here until the most recent heir decided to preserve it permanently as a museum. Perhaps its most stunning architectural feature is the elliptical staircase that swirls upward from ground level to the top floor. There is a prominent nautical theme befitting the history of the family.

The quirkiest and most surprising element of the Forbes House is its collection focused on Abraham Lincoln. A Forbes descendent, Mary Bowditch Forbes, revered President Lincoln. She amassed a large collection

Elizabeth S. Levy Merrick

of Lincoln memorabilia and actually had built
cabin birthplace, which still stands on the ground. ...plica of his log
There is spacious parkland around the house itsei.
and open lawn make for an enjoyable stroll (or picnic i..ve of pines
The vista from the street side of the property includes fields,weather).
the Boston skyline in the distance. After your visit, be sure to es, and
the street in order to meander through Governor Hutchinson's Fi cross
field is a property of the Trustees of Reservations and is free to all.he
sloping field belonged to the last royal governor of the Massachuset.
Bay Colony before the revolution. It is lovely in all seasons and affords a
spectacular view of Boston Harbor and the city itself.

To Visit

Location: 215 Adams Street, Milton, MA 02186

Opening hours: Year-round. Tours by reservation only, on Wednesdays, Saturdays, and Sundays at 1:00 p.m. and 3:00 p.m. Call ahead to confirm tour times as tours are suspended during special events and to make your reservation.

Type of tour: Guided.

Admission fees: $10/adults, $8/seniors and students, children under age five are free.

Directions by car: From Boston, take I-93 South to exit 10 (Squantum Street/Milton). Merge onto Squantum Street, then take a right onto Adams Street. Follow Adams Street for about a mile. The Forbes House will be on your left.

Parking: Parking is available in driveway and parking lot.

Directions by public transportation: It is possible to get to the Forbes House Museum by public transportation, although it will not be quick. From Boston, take the MBTA Red Line to Ashmont Station. Then catch the Mattapan High Speed Rail Line westbound, and get off at Milton Station. Walk about a half mile south on Adams Street.

More info. nis property is owned by the Forbes House Charitable Trust. We w.forbeshousemuseum.org Phone 617-696-1815

Elizabeth S. Levy Merrick

GIBSON HOUSE MUSEUM

Boston, Massachusetts

Year Built: 1860

What's Special: *Perfectly preserved Victorian townhouse; original family furnishings throughout; glimpse into life of prosperous Back Bay family*

If you have ever wondered what lies behind the elegant facades of Back Bay's Victorian townhouses, the Gibson House is for you. It is one of the rare row houses that remains intact as a single living unit and provides an authentic picture of how well-to-do families lived years ago in these lovely residences.

This five-story, Italian Renaissance townhouse was built by a wealthy widow, Catherine Hammond Gibson, just before the start of the Civil War. The Back Bay was still being filled in, adding much new land to the city, and developing into the elegant neighborhood it ultimately became. The house was designed by Boston architect Edward Clarke Cabot, who also designed the acclaimed Boston Athenaeum. The Gibson family had prospered in the merchant trade. Several generations of the family lived here, and Charles Gibson Jr. not only left the house to be maintained as a museum but also helped to start this transformation before his death in 1954. His foresight and interest in preservation meant that the house remains as a testament to life in the Victorian era.

Dim lighting reminiscent of the gaslight era greets visitors in the impressive entry hall with its black-walnut woodwork and original gold-foil wallpaper. Decorative arches and graceful, arched doorways are a recurrent motif throughout the house. The rooms are filled with the richness and detail characteristic of Victorian style. In the narrow townhouse, living spaces are stacked vertically. The first floor contains the dining room, with its impressive chandelier. The elegant parlor and library are on the second floor. Charles Gibson Jr.'s study—filled with family mementos and literary paraphernalia reflecting his identity as a poet—as well as a bedroom, are on the third floor. Original furnishings owned by the family are found throughout the house. Below stairs are an original kitchen and laundry room that provide an understanding of how servants worked to keep the household running. The fourth and fifth floors (servants' and children's rooms) are not open to the public.

The Gibson House has several other interesting features, including a central heating shaft that allowed heat to travel upstairs more efficiently—an innovative feature at the time. It also has the only original coal shed remaining in the Back Bay.

Allow yourself extra time before or after your visit to wander along streets filled with townhouses from the same era as the Gibson House. You will be all the more delighted at discovering the hidden history within.

To Visit

Location: 137 Beacon St, Boston, MA 02116

Opening hours: Year-round, Wednesday through Sunday. Tours start at 1:00, 2:00, and 3:00 p.m. Closed New Year's Day, Fourth of July, Thanksgiving Day, and Christmas Day.

Type of tour: Guided.

Admission fees: $9/adults, $6/seniors and students, $3/ children under twelve.

Directions by car: This house is on Beacon Street, a main thoroughfare in downtown Boston. It is located between Arlington and Berkeley Streets.

Parking: Limited on-street parking, often difficult to find open spots. There are public parking garages in the area. It is easiest to take public transportation.

Elizabeth S. Levy Merrick

Directions by public transportation: The closest MBTA station is Arlington Station on the Green Line. The house is a very short walk from there.

More information: This property is owned by the Gibson Society, Inc. Website: www.thegibsonhouse.org Phone: 617-267-6338

GORE PLACE

Waltham, Massachusetts

Year Built: 1806

What's Special: *Stunningly designed and furnished rooms; very large mansion and spacious grounds; home of former Massachusetts governor; servants' quarters included in tour*

Gore Place is an imposing brick mansion still surrounded by extensive grounds and open fields. With fifty rooms, it is one of the largest historic houses open to the public in the Boston area. It was the home of Massachusetts Governor Christopher Gore and his wife, Rebecca, who played an active role in designing the mansion along the lines of an elegant English country house.

When the house was built in 1806, Waltham was a two-hour carriage ride from Boston—country rather than town. The Gores created a home that is a wonderland of elegant public rooms and luxurious private spaces. The entry hall welcomes visitors with a swirling spiral staircase and twenty-foot ceilings. The oval hall, or ballroom, has its original marble floor, built on a cushion of horsehair to make dancing more comfortable. The drawing room is also oval-shaped, has bird-patterned wallpaper, and is filled with light-reflecting crystal, as is much of the house. This enhances the airy, fluid, and elegant impression given to visitors today, just as in the Gores' time.

The house is plentifully furnished with period antiques, including some Gore family possessions. Rooms are set up to suggest life in the house during the family's occupancy. Thus, you will see food set out on

Elizabeth S. Levy Merrick

the dining room table ready for guests to enjoy. Naturally, to maintain such a home required servants. The servants' quarters are tucked away on a mezzanine level that is invisible from the outside. The servants' stories are told as well, including that of the remarkable butler. He was a free black man who wrote a book on running such a household.

Gore Place is stunning and fascinating to visit anytime. But if you have an opportunity to take the "Full Moon Tour," do so! This is an evening tour typically offered monthly to coincide with the full moon. It is conducted by costumed guides who lead visitors through candlelit (or otherwise pleasantly illuminated) rooms. From the moment you leave your car behind and follow the path by lantern light to the front door, it is a magical experience you will not forget.

There is also a small farm at Gore Place, which produces fruits, vegetables, meat, and eggs. These products are sold at a farmer's market on the estate grounds during the warmer months, and proceeds benefit the farm.

To Visit

Location: 52 Gore Street, Waltham, MA 02453

Opening hours: Year-round. Guided tours Monday through Friday at 1:00 p.m. and Saturdays at 12:00, 1:00, 2:00, and 3:00 p.m.

Type of tour: Guided.

Admission fees: $12/adults, $6/ children five to twelve. Gore Place members free.

Directions by car: From Boston, take I-90/Massachusetts Turnpike west and then take exit 17 to Watertown Square. Turn left onto Route 20 (Main Street). Travel 1.25 miles to Gore Street. From Route 128/I-95 exit 26 to Route 20 east (Main Street), for 3.5 miles to Gore Street.

Parking: Ample parking lot.

Directions by public transportation: Take the MBTA Red Line to Central Square Station. At the bus stop at intersection of Green and Magazine Streets, take the #70 bus (Cedarwood via Watertown). Get off at the Warren Street stop. Gore Place is just a few minutes' walk from there.

More information: This property is owned by the Gore Place Society. Website: www.goreplace.org Phone: 781- 894-2798

Elizabeth S. Levy Merrick

HANCOCK-CLARKE HOUSE

Lexington, Massachusetts

Year Built: 1737

What's Special: Important Revolutionary War connections; beautifully restored eighteenth-century house with seventeenth-century section

The Hancock-Clarke House was the home of John Hancock's grandfather, and John Hancock spent time here as a child. But the house is most famed for its role in the events of April 18, 1775, during Paul Revere's midnight ride.

At the time of the revolution, Reverend Jonas Clarke lived in this house, which served as a parsonage. He supported the patriot cause. Samuel Adams and John Hancock were staying here on that fateful evening. Paul Revere came to the house to warn Adams and Hancock of British regulars on the move, which enabled them to avoid capture and attend the Continental Congress in Philadelphia soon thereafter.

The house actually consists of two houses joined together. It has been beautifully restored in recent years and is an extremely handsome example of the architecture of its time. Among the rooms on view are those in which Hancock and Adams slept and spent time. The paneled dining room has its original table and chairs. Richly carved moldings, Delft tiles, and original flowered wall hangings dating to the 1700s are among the special features of this house. There is also an excellent orientation film on the beginning of the revolution, as well as a colonial herb garden.

The Hancock-Clarke House deserves a spot on your agenda for historic sightseeing in the Lexington-Concord area.

To Visit

Location: 36 Hancock Street, Lexington, MA 02420

Opening hours: April–Memorial Day, weekends 10:00 a.m.–4:00 p.m. Memorial Day–October, daily 10:00 a.m.–4:00 p.m. Tours hourly.

Type of tour: Guided.

Admission fees: $7/adult, $5/child. Or purchase the First Shot! Package (admission to three historic houses): $12/adult, $8/child. Child rate is for ages six to sixteen, children under six are free.

Directions by car: From Boston, take Route 93 north to exit 37B to merge onto I-95/Route 128 South. Get off at exit 31A to merge onto MA-225 E/MA-4 S/ Bedford Street in Lexington. In about half a mile, turn left onto North Hancock Street, then stay straight through the traffic rotary to continue onto Hancock Street.

Parking: Free parking on site.

Directions by public transportation: From Boston, (Monday–Saturday) take the MBTA Red Line to Alewife Station. Bus routes #76 (Hanscom Air Force Base) and #62 (Bedford VA Hospital) run to and from Alewife Station. Buses run frequently during peak hours, traveling along Massachusetts Avenue and making stops in Lexington Center. The house is also within walking distance of Buckman Tavern and Lexington Center.

More information: This property is owned by the Lexington Historical Society. Website: www.lexingtonhistory.org Phone: 781-862-1703

Elizabeth S. Levy Merrick

JAMES BLAKE HOUSE

Dorchester (Boston), Massachusetts

Year Built: c. 1661

What's Special: *Oldest house in Boston; unusual construction methods for the region*

The James Blake House has the distinction of being the oldest house in Boston. It is one of three historic house museums owned by the Dorchester Historical Society. Opening hours are the same for all of them, making it easy to visit all of them on one day if you choose. This trio of houses is outside of the downtown areas most frequented by tourists, and these houses are not as well-known as they should be even by Boston-area residents. Therefore, you can expect to enjoy your visit without a great deal of company.

Built in the mid-seventeenth century, the James Blake House was originally the farmhouse home of James and Elizabeth Blake and their family. James Blake was a prosperous farmer and became prominent in church and civic affairs. He was a deacon of his church and held public office, including as deputy to the Massachusetts General Court.

An interesting feature of this house is that it was built using methods of construction common to the West Country of England, namely heavy timber-framing construction rather than brick and plaster. This was unusual in this area. Another curious fact about the house is that throughout the eighteenth century, separate families lived in the two halves of the house. In 1895 the house was moved by the Dorchester Historical Society from its original location nearby to save it from demolition.

Elizabeth S. Levy Merrick

Today, the James Blake House is inhabited by a caretaker, and it feels like a contemporary person's living space in a very old building. It is unlikely you will feel thoroughly transported into the past here, but you will find much of interest in this ancient house, its construction, and the pure fact of its survival to this day.

To Visit

Location: 735 Columbia Road (Richardson Park) Dorchester, MA 02125

Opening hours: Year-round, third Sunday of each month, 11:00 a.m.–4:00 p.m.

Type of tour: Guided.

Admission fees: Donation requested.

Directions by car: From downtown Boston, take I-93 to the Columbia/JFK exit #15. The exit ramp takes you to Columbia Road. Turn right on Columbia Road and proceed through the second traffic light. The Blake House is several blocks down on the left.

Parking: Street parking is available.

Directions by public transportation: Take the MBTA Red Line to the JFK/UMass Station. When you come out of the station, turn left on Columbia Road, go under the Expressway and walk five or six long blocks. You will see the Blake House on the left.

More information: This property is owned by the Dorchester Historical Society. Website: www.dorchesterhistoricalsociety.org Phone: 617-293-3052

Elizabeth S. Levy Merrick

JASON RUSSELL HOUSE

Arlington, Massachusetts

Year Built: 1740

What's special: Site of Revolutionary War battle; early eighteenth-century farmhouse origins with later addition; local-history museum in part of the house; relatively undiscovered

Set back from busy Massachusetts Avenue in Arlington Center stands the Jason Russell House. It is a substantial farmhouse of which the original two rooms date to 1740. This structure is a physical reminder not only of New England's colonial and agricultural past but of the key events that took place on April 19, 1775. The Battle of Menotomy (the earlier name for this area) raged in the house and yard of this now-peaceful spot. The fighting in Menotomy has been called the bloodiest in the first day of the Revolutionary War. Yet, while droves of tourists flock to Lexington and Concord (which fully deserve the heavy visitation), the Battle of Menotomy in general and the Jason Russell house in particular receive far less attention.

The Jason Russell House is named after the farmer who owned this house in 1775. The British regulars were retreating to Boston after the battles at Lexington and Concord. Russell was killed—shot and bayoneted—by British soldiers on his own doorstep. Eleven other patriots (many from the militias of towns further afield, such as Danvers and Lynn) were killed in the yard or house; two redcoats also were killed.

This is a must-see for Revolutionary War buffs. As you walk through the rooms of this house, including the dark kitchen where Mrs. Russell found the bodies of her husband and compatriots when she returned after the battle, it is easy to picture the historic events that took place here. The bullet holes are still visible in the house. At the same time, it is informative and interesting as a time capsule illustrating life on an eighteenth-century farm, as well as the following century, due to additions and changes. The house is extensively furnished with eighteenth- and nineteenth-century furniture and objects, many belonging to the Russell family, which occupied the house until 1896.

In addition to guided tours, admission to the house includes a small museum with exhibits focused on local Arlington history. It is interesting to see artifacts that show the evolution of the town up to the present time. You can also walk a few minutes to the Old Burying Ground where Jason Russell and those who died with him are buried. This historic cemetery is worth a visit in its own right.

To Visit

Location: 7 Jason Street, Arlington, MA 02476

Opening hours: Patriots Day (mid-April) through Columbus Day (mid-October). Saturdays and Sundays, 1:00–4:00 p.m.

Type of tour: Guided.

Admission fees: $5/adults, $2/child.

Directions by car: From Boston, take Storrow Drive, continue on Soldiers Field Road, then bear right onto Route 16 (Fresh Pond Parkway) toward Cambridge (you will see signs for Route 16/Route 2). Stay on Route 16 until you get to the intersection with Massachusetts Avenue. Turn left onto Massachusetts Avenue heading west toward Arlington. In Arlington Center, turn left onto Jason Street.

Parking: Parking is located on Jason Street, or take the next right onto Jason Terrace where there is a parking lot.

Directions by public transportation: From Boston, take the MBTA Red Line to Porter Square Station. Take the #77 Arlington Heights bus from stop on

Massachusetts Avenue in Porter Square. Get off in Arlington Center opposite Town Hall and walk one block west on Massachusetts Avenue to Jason Street.

More Information: This house is owned by the Arlington Historical Society. Website: www.arlingtonhistorical.org Phone: 781-648-4300

Lemuel Clap House

Dorchester (Boston), Massachusetts

Year Built: c. 1710, enlarged in 1767

What's Special: Well-preserved eighteenth-century house; interesting artifacts

The Lemuel Clap house is a substantial two-story, wood-framed house. The house owes its current appearance to extensive remodeling and enlargement dating to 1767, which reflects the symmetry of Georgian-style architecture. It stands adjacent to the William Clapp house, residence of Lemuel Clap's son.

Captain Lemuel Clap was among several generations of the family who were in the tannery business. A millstone in the front yard is thought to possibly come from their tannery nearby. Clap was a captain in the Continental Army during the revolution.

The house has mostly original woodwork and some original glass windows. There are numerous rooms, including an elegant parlor, added during the 1760s renovation, which contains an item of the wedding furniture (a table) belonging to Captain Clap and his second wife, Rebecca.

There is also an interesting "borning room" off of the original kitchen area. It was a warm space that could be used for a birthing room as well as taking care of sick family members.

The house contains furnishings and artifacts from a range of time periods. These include an exhibit of samplers and other embroidery. A unique bed with ornate geometric carving is rumored to have been made from pieces of Minot House, a colonial house vanished long ago.

Elizabeth S. Levy Merrick

Industrial buildings now loom to the back of the house, but in front there is a lovely yard with vintage flower varieties. It is hard to believe that there were still orchards here up to the 1950s and dairy operations until the 1940s.

Seeing the Lemuel Clap House and the William Clapp House together makes the most sense. Start at the William Clapp House to get an overview of Dorchester history. It is also easy to fit in the third Dorchester Historical Society house museum, the James Blake House, which is a short walk from here.

To Visit

Location: 199 Boston Street, Dorchester, MA 02125

Opening hours: Year-round, third Sunday of the month, 1:00–4:00 p.m.

Type of tour: Guided.

Admission fees: Donations welcome.

Directions by car: From Boston, take I-93 South to exit 18 toward Massachusetts Avenue/Roxbury/Andrew Square. Take a slight left onto I-93 Frontage Rd. Then take a slight right toward Boston Street. Turn right onto Boston Street. House is on the right.

Parking: Street parking is available

Directions by public transportation: Take MBTA Red Line to toward Ashmont, and get off at Andrew Square Station. Walk from Andrew Square Station (note, part of the route is somewhat industrial) or take the #17 Fields Corner via Kane Square bus, getting off on Boston Street at Harvest Street.

More Information: This property is owned by the Dorchester Historical Society. Website: www.dorchesterhistoricalsociety.org Phone: 617-293-3052

Elizabeth S. Levy Merrick

LONGFELLOW HOUSE-WASHINGTON'S HEADQUARTERS

Cambridge, Massachusetts

Year Built: 1759

What's Special: *Major historical and literary significance; Revolutionary War connection; elegant mansion; Longfellow family furnishings; lovely gardens*

The Longfellow House-Washington's Headquarters is located on Brattle Street (known as Tory Row in colonial times), one of the most beautiful streets in Massachusetts. Many historic houses line this leafy thoroughfare that begins in Harvard Square, but the Longfellow House stands out. This house museum will enchant lovers of American history, literature, and architecture. The large and beautiful Georgian mansion tells the story of two American icons: famed poet and scholar Henry Wadsworth Longfellow and George Washington, hero of the American Revolution and the nation's first president. This house should be toward the top of any must-see list of major house museums in the Boston area.

The house brims over with beauty and history. It was built by a loyalist family that fled the revolution. Washington made it his headquarters when he arrived in July 1775 to lead the Continental Army. Many years later, in 1837, Longfellow rented rooms in the house. When Longfellow married Fanny Appleton in 1843, her father gave the couple the house as a wedding gift. It has been restored to pristine condition, with large and opulently furnished rooms in the style of Longfellow's day. Longfellow's study in which he wrote was also the room where Washington conducted much of his business. The richly furnished parlor has a lovely chandelier, marble-topped table, and original wallpaper from the Longfellows' time. The library was the scene of a terrible tragedy, in which Fanny Longfellow fell victim to a household fire (her clothing caught fire, perhaps from a candle) and later died. A branching central staircase leads to the second floor, where numerous bedrooms are also open to the public.

Because this is a National Historic Site owned by the National Park Service, house tours are given by park rangers. As is typical of park ranger guides, they are highly knowledgeable and engaging and help to bring the house to life. Furthermore, many portraits of Longfellow family members and friends—including noteworthy figures, such as Nathaniel Hawthorne—hang in the rooms, so that visitors will feel immersed in the life and relationships that went on here.

Spacious formal gardens and parkland surround the house. If you visit in the spring or summer, you will find a glorious profusion of roses, peonies, and other flowers blooming brilliantly along the geometric paths. Relax under the pergola or in a sunny spot to savor this lovely scene.

To Visit

Location: 105 Brattle Street, Cambridge, MA 02138

Opening hours: Late May through late October, Wednesday through Sunday, with guided tours on the hour between 10:00 a.m. and 4:00 p.m. Last tour at 4:00 p.m.

Type of tour: Guided.

Admission fees: Admission is free. (This is the bargain of the century considering what is to be seen here.)

Directions by car: From Boston: Take Storrow Drive west, and continue on Soldiers Field Road. Take the exit, bearing to the right, for Route 16/ Route 2/Route 3/Fresh Pond Parkway. After about half a mile, take a right onto Brattle Street. The house will be on the left, 0.8 miles.

Parking: Metered parking on the street, but note it can be difficult to find parking spots. There are parking garages in Harvard Square. The only onsite parking is reserved for visitors with disabilities.

Directions by public transportation: Take the MBTA Red Line to Harvard Square Station. Take the Church Street exit out of the station, and walk down Church Street to Brattle Street. Take a right onto Brattle Street. The house is on the right, about a ten-minute walk down Brattle Street.

More information: This property is owned by the National Park Service. Website: www.nps.gov Phone: 617-876-4491

LORING-GREENOUGH HOUSE

Jamaica Plain (Boston), Massachusetts

Year Built: 1760

What's Special: *Last surviving Georgian estate in Jamaica Plain; Revolutionary War military hospital*

The Loring-Greenough House is a local landmark in the Jamaica Plain section of Boston. However, it is often overlooked by out-of-town visitors and even area residents. A solid Georgian mansion with a picturesque Captain's Walk, situated on a pleasant two acres, it serves as a popular venue for community events, such as concerts and fairs. It is also easy to see why it is often rented for weddings, with gracious rooms on the first floor.

The house was originally built as a country estate by a wealthy Tory family, the Lorings, who fled the revolution. The property was a patriot military hospital at the time of the Battle of Bunker Hill and served other military uses. Later the property was in the Greenough family for multiple generations.

The large public rooms downstairs reflect various time periods. The original Great Hall is now three separate rooms, with lovely moldings and period details. There are period furnishings which are not original to the house. Upstairs, there are furnished bedrooms and sitting rooms. The Loring-Greenough House contains several interesting collections, including calling card cases of every design and material, hair combs, and embroidered samplers. Another feature of interest is the old summer kitchen, in an attached building.

Elizabeth S. Levy Merrick

No discussion of the Loring-Greenough House can be complete without noting the Tuesday Club. In 1896 the Jamaica Plain Tuesday Club was founded by a group of women who aimed to promote cultural life and establish the club as a philanthropic and educational organization. The Tuesday Club purchased the property in 1924 and enabled this special place to be preserved for future generations. Happily, the Tuesday Club thrives to this day and continues its stewardship of the Loring-Greenough House as well as its civic-minded mission.

To Visit

Location: 12 South Street, Jamaica Plain, MA 02130

Opening hours: April–December, guided tours on Sundays, 1:00–3:00 p.m. January–March, tours by appointment only.

Type of tour: Guided.

Admission fees: Requested donation $5/adults, $2/school-age children

Directions by car: From downtown Boston, one option is to take Route I-93 South to exit 18, Massachusetts Avenue toward Roxbury/Andrew Square. Stay straight to go onto the Massachusetts Avenue Connector, which then becomes Melnea Cass Boulevard. Go 0.4 miles and turn left onto Harrison Avenue. Turn right onto Dudley Street. After 0.1. miles, turn slight left onto Washington Street. In 1.7 miles, turn right onto Green Street. Turn left onto Centre Street. In 0.3 miles, take slight left onto South Street. The Loring-Greenough House is on the left.

Parking: Parking lot next to house or street parking.

Directions by public transportation: Take the MBTA Orange Line to Forest Hills Station. Take the #39 bus (Back Bay Station via Copley Square) and get off at the intersection of South Street and Sedgwick Street at the Civil War Monument in Jamaica Plain. The bus stop is in front of the house.

More information: This property is owned by the Jamaica Plain Tuesday Club, Inc. Website: www.loring-greenough.org Phone: 617-524-3158

Elizabeth S. Levy Merrick

LYMAN ESTATE

Waltham, Massachusetts

Year Built: 1793

What's Special: Spectacular mansion with extensive, landscaped grounds; built by well-known architect Samuel McIntyre

Prepare to fall in love with the Lyman Estate (also called "The Vale"). Set far back from the road, down a long driveway, the lavender-painted, three-story mansion with a side portico proclaims elegance and wealth. Originally the country estate of a successful shipping magnate and industrialist, the early Federal-style mansion was extensively added to in later years. The end result is a very large house comprised of one exquisite room after another.

Prominent architect Samuel McIntyre designed the house. It is filled with delightful design flourishes, such as multiple archways and an ornate staircase. Especially appealing spaces include the oval room, with gracefully curved doors and windows, and the grand ballroom. The Lyman Estate was clearly built for large-scale entertaining as well as for family interludes.

It is not only the mansion that makes this property shine. The landscaped grounds share pride of place. There are thirty-seven acres of open lawns, gardens, and parkland to enjoy. This ensures that the view from every window in the house is beautiful and also provides restorative space to stroll or sit outdoors. Many weddings take place here at the arched Greek temple-like structure surrounded by flourishing gardens with Joe Pye Weed, black-eyed Susans, and other New England flowers dancing in the breeze.

To top off any visit to the Lyman Estate, you must also visit the greenhouses, which are among the oldest in the country. Wander through several adjoining greenhouses filled with camellias, orchids, and many other types of plants. It is a special treat in cool weather. Many plants are for sale, along with Lyman Estate memorabilia.

The Lyman Estate is an oasis of beauty and peacefulness with an abundance of attractions. It absolutely warrants a visit, even if you need to go out of your way to do so. And although it is lovely in any season, visiting when the gardens are at their height will make your visit extra-special.

To Visit

Location: 185 Lyman St., Waltham, MA 02452

Opening hours: Year-round, third Saturday of every month, 10:00 a.m.–1:00 p.m. Guided tours on the hour, last tour at noon. Check the website or call ahead to make sure the estate is not closed for a private function on the day you are planning to visit. Closed most major holidays.

Type of tour: Guided.

Admission fees: $5/ adults, $4/seniors. Free for Historic New England members and Waltham residents.

Directions by car: From Boston, take I-90 (Mass Pike) West. Get off at exit 17 (Watertown) to merge onto Centre Street in Newton. Continue onto Galen Street, then continue onto MA-16 East/Mount Auburn Street. At Watertown Square, turn left onto Main Street and proceed 2.6 miles into Waltham. Turn right onto Lyman Street. At rotary, go partway around then bear right through stone pillar down the gravel driveway of the Lyman Estate on Beaver Street.

Parking: Ample parking lot just beyond the house.

Directions by public transportation: Take the MBTA Red Line to Alewife Station. Take bus #554 Waverly-Newton Corner-Mass Pike. Get off at Beaver Street and Valley View Road. The Lyman Estate is a five-minute walk down Beaver Street to the Lyman Estate driveway.

More information: This property is owned by Historic New England. Website: www.historicnewengland.org Phone: 617-994-5912

Munroe Tavern

Lexington, Massachusetts

Year Built: 1735

What's Special: *Revolutionary War field hospital for redcoats; story told from British point of view*

M unroe Tavern is unique in the Lexington-Concord sphere of American Revolution sites in presenting events from the British point of view. Start your visit with the excellent video to provide context. It is fascinating to hear the founding story of the nation described as a treasonous rebellion by upstart American colonists.

British regulars, retreating back to Boston on that momentous day in April 1775, took over this house. It served as a field hospital; the house was likely filled with British officers. There is an interesting exhibit of reproduction eighteenth-century medical instruments, which will evoke terror in anyone seriously contemplating the state of medical care at that time.

The Munroe family, owners of the tavern (which was also their home), were patriots. The head of the household was a member of the Lexington militia, active in events that day, and his wife and children fled their home. There were numerous members of the extended Munroe family on Lexington Green that day. This is also a place where President George Washington ate, if not slept. The artifacts of his 1789 visit are on display, including the spoon, cup, and chair that he used.

Like many of the historic sites in Lexington and Concord, this is a spot filled with history and beauty. Outside there is a garden filled with flowers typically grown here two hundred years ago, lovingly maintained by garden club volunteers.

To fully savor the Munroe Tavern experience, stop in for refreshments when the Tea Room is open. And take advantage of the proximity of other house museums in town by purchasing a combination ticket that also includes Buckman Tavern and the Hancock-Clarke House.

To Visit

Location: 1332 Massachusetts Avenue, Lexington, MA 02420

Opening hours: April–May, open weekends; June-October, daily, 12:00–4:00 p.m., tours hourly. Tea Room open Saturdays and Sundays from 12:00 p.m. till 4:00 p.m.

Type of tour: Guided.

Admission fees: $7/adult, $5/child (ages six to sixteen), children under six are free. Members of the Lexington Historical Society receive free admission. (Note the "First Shot!" package provides admission to three historic houses—Munroe Tavern, Buckman Tavern, Hancock-Clarke House: $12/adult, $8/child.)

Directions by car: The house is located near the center of Lexington. You can reach Lexington via Route 95/128 (exit 31A, Bedford Street/Rt. 225) and Route 2 (Waltham Street exit). Follow the signs to Lexington Center. The house is about one mile east of Lexington Center.

Parking: Parking lot and street parking available.

Directions by public transportation: Take the MBTA Red Line to Alewife Station. At the Alewife busway, get the #62/76 bus for Bedford VA via Lexington Center-Hanscom AFB. Get off at Massachusetts Avenue and Percey Road.

More information: This property is owned by the Lexington Historical Society. Website: www.lexingtonhistory.org Phone: 781-862-1703

Elizabeth S. Levy Merrick

NICHOLS HOUSE MUSEUM

Boston, Massachusetts

Year Built: 1804

What's Special: *Home of pioneering female landscape designer and social reformer; Beacon Hill location; building attributed to architect Charles Bulfinch*

B eacon Hill is among the most charming, well-preserved, and historic neighborhoods in the country. Any stroll along its narrow streets lined with venerable brick townhouses will inspire you to curiosity about what these houses are like inside, but it is hard to find ones that are open to the public and still have original interiors. Fortunately, there is a notable exception: Nichols House. There you will be welcomed into the past and into the home of a truly remarkable woman, Rose Standish Nichols.

The Nichols family bought the home in 1885. Rose Nichols's father was a physician, and what is now the library was originally Dr. Nichols's consulting room where he saw patients. Rose Standish Nichols was educated in a very progressive fashion for that time. She was one of the first female landscape designers and writers on that topic and was a graduate of the Massachusetts Institute of Technology at a time when extremely few women attended college. She was also a pacifist, founding an international peace organization, and suffragist in the movement to obtain the vote for women. She never married, and her home was a gathering place for intellectuals who liked to mix substantive debate and conversation with their afternoon tea. Rose Nichols was also a gifted artist whose creations include embroidered bed hangings and skillfully carved chairs, all on display.

The house is a very comfortable and spacious one that still feels like a home, rather than a place meant primarily to impress. There is a graceful spiral staircase and many lovely rooms to enjoy. All of the furnishings and objects in the house are original to the family, many collected during the family's trips to Europe. In fact, the entire house has been maintained to look just as it did when Rose Standish Nichols died in 1960 and left it as a museum.

By the time you leave Nichols House, you will feel as though you had known Rose yourself and were part of the active intellectual and artistic life of Boston during the late nineteenth and early twentieth century. Her spirit seems to still inhabit these spaces, welcoming you into her circle.

To Visit

Location: 55 Mount Vernon Street, Boston, MA 02108

Opening hours: April 1–October 31, Tuesday–Saturday, 11:00 a.m.–4:00 p.m. November 1–March 31, Thursday–Saturday, 11:00 a.m.–4:00 p.m. Tours on the half hour, last tour at 4:00 p.m.

Type of tour: Guided.

Admission fees: $8/adults. Children twelve and under free.

Directions by car: House is in downtown Boston, in the Beacon Hill section of the city.

Parking: There is street parking in the area, but it can be very difficult to find available spots. There are parking garages underneath Boston Common and on nearby Cambridge Street.

Directions by public transportation: Take the MBTA Red Line to Park Street Station. Walk up Park Street toward the Massachusetts State House to Beacon Street. Follow Beacon Street until you reach Walnut Street on your right. Follow Walnut Street, and turn right on Mount Vernon Street.

Elizabeth S. Levy Merrick

More information: This property is owned by the Nichols House Museum. Website: www.nicholshousemuseum.org Phone: 617-227-6993

THE OLD MANSE

Concord, Massachusetts

Year Built: 1770

What's Special: Home of Ralph Waldo Emerson and Nathaniel Hawthorne; situated in well-preserved historic landscape

Those who know and appreciate the literary genius of Ralph Waldo Emerson and Nathaniel Hawthorne cannot fail to visit the Old Manse. Concord in general, and this house in particular, was a nineteenth-century hub for numerous authors and others who subscribed to the philosophy of Transcendentalism. But the Old Manse is also compelling to anyone who simply relishes the somewhat sleepy, lost-in-time feel of many old New England houses—for this is one par excellence.

The short, tree-lined gravel path leads from the road to the front door of this Georgian house just as it did in the 1800s. Modest-size rooms are pleasant and comfortable. Emerson owned the house and wrote his acclaimed work *Nature* here. He later rented the Old Manse to Hawthorne and his wife, Sophia. Hawthorne wrote *Mosses from an Old Manse* in the same room where Emerson had worked, at a desk that another intellectual giant, Henry David Thoreau, built. The book, which is available at the excellent bookstore and gift shop here, consists of essays that center around the Old Manse and the time Hawthorne spent here. It is a wonderful experience to visit the house and then read Hawthorne's account. For her part, Sophia Hawthorne left a very literal mark on the house: an etching on windowpane, cut with a diamond.

Elizabeth S. Levy Merrick

The Old Manse has spacious grounds including a large vegetable garden, which has been restored to the way Thoreau had originally planted it as a wedding gift to the Hawthornes. It is situated in a bucolic landscape of fields, stone walls, and the Concord River. The property adjoins a section of Minuteman National Historical Park and is just a few minutes' walk to the iconic North Bridge, site of battle on April 19, 1775.

There is so much of historical interest to see and do in Concord that the town is an ideal spot to immerse yourself in the past for several days or even a leisurely week if you are so inclined. Of course, this extraordinary concentration of historic sites can also make for a series of delightful day trips. However you plan your time here in Concord, the Old Manse will surely be a highlight.

To Visit

Location: 269 Monument St., Concord, MA 01742

Opening hours: Mid-March–late May, Saturday and Sunday, 12:00 –5:00 p.m. Late May–October, Tuesday–Sunday, 12:00 –5:00 p.m. November–December, Saturday and Sunday, 12:00–5:00 p.m. Prebooked, by-prior-appointment tours are also available year-round, seven days a week.

Type of tour: Guided.

Admission fees: Admission free to members of Trustees of Reservations. Nonmembers: Adult $8/adults; $5/children (six to twelve); $7/seniors and students (with valid ID); $25/family (two adults and up to three minor children).

Directions by car: From Boston, take Storrow Drive, continue on Soldiers Field Road to Eliot Bridge. Take US 3/Alewife Brook Parkway and follow through two traffic rotaries. Turn left onto Route 2 West. Where Route 2 takes a sharp left, continue straight onto Cambridge Turnpike. At end, turn left onto Lexington Road to Concord Center. Turn right to take Monument St. north 0.5 mi.

Parking: Parking lot next to house.

Directions by public transportation: From Boston, take the MBTA Green Line to North Station. At North Station, take the commuter rail Fitchburg/South Acton Line-Fitchburg, and get off at Concord Station. The Old Manse is more than a mile from the train station.

More information: This property is owned by the Trustees of Reservations. Website: www.thetrustees.org Phone: 978-369-3909

Elizabeth S. Levy Merrick

ORCHARD HOUSE

Concord, Massachusetts

Year Built: 1690 with 1720 addition

What's Special: *Home of author Louisa May Alcott; place where* Little Women *was written and set*

Crowds of Louisa May Alcott fans make the pilgrimage to Orchard House: young girls who love *Little Women* and adults with fond memories of her books from their own childhood. Orchard House also draws those with a more general interest in nineteenth-century American literature. Louisa May Alcott is of particular interest because she was a woman ahead of her time who resisted some of the conventional restrictions placed upon women. Indeed, this was a very progressive household in many respects. As a result of its popularity, this is one of the few houses featured in this book at which you will quite possibly have a bit of a wait for your tour.

Orchard House is picturesque and nestled into a hillside. The Alcotts created the current structure by joining together two houses, one dating to 1690. The colonial vintage of the house is not a focus of the visit, however, particularly given many changes made to it subsequently. Your tour begins with viewing an interesting short video. Although tours are limited to fifteen visitors, several of the rooms are very small (including the room in which you watch the video) and can feel crowded—so this tour is not for the claustrophobic. However, for the Louisa May Alcott fan, there is no substitute for seeing where the author actually wrote and set the classic novel *Little Women*. You will see the "mood pillow" that Alcott's heroine,

Jo (modeled after herself), used to signal her frame of mind, observe the spot where their family plays were performed, learn about all of the Alcott family members, and see the endearing owl collection in Louisa's bedroom.

This is a comfortable, middle-class home. Its main appeal by far is that it was the Alcotts' home for almost two decades. Actually, it was their twenty-third home. Louisa's father, Bronson Alcott, was brilliant but not known for his ability to maintain steady work and bring in sufficient income for his family. Students of the Alcotts' history might, in fact, feel that the Orchard House tours somewhat gloss over the very rough edges of the Alcott family story. Nonetheless, most Alcott fans who make this pilgrimage are likely to leave feeling good about visiting a place that brings *Little Women* even more to life.

To Visit

Location: 399 Lexington Rd., Concord, MA 01742

Opening hours: November 1–March 31, Monday–Friday, 11:00–3:00 p.m. (last tour at 3:00), Saturday, 10:00 a.m.–4:30 p.m., Sunday, 1:00–4:30 p.m. (last tour at 4:30 p.m.). April 1–October 31, Monday–Saturday, 10:00 a.m.–4:30 p.m., Sunday, 1:00 p.m.–4:30 p.m. (last tour at 4:30 p.m.). Closed on Easter, Thanksgiving, Christmas, and January 1 and 2; open at 12:00 p.m. on Patriots Day (third Monday in April).

Type of tour: Guided.

Admission fees: $10/adults; $8/seniors (sixty-two years and up) and college students (with ID); $5/youths (ages six to seventeen); children under six and members, free; $25/family rate (two adults and up to four youths)

Directions by car: From Boston, take Storrow Drive, continuing on Soldiers Field Road to Eliot Bridge, following signs for MA-2/US-3/Arlington/Fresh Pond Parkway. Follow Fresh Pond Parkway and Alewife Brook Parkway to intersection with Route 2. Make a left onto Route 2 West. Where Route 2 takes a sharp left, stay straight and continue onto Cambridge Turnpike. In 0.7 miles, turn right onto Hawthorne Lane, then make a sharp left onto Lexington Road. Orchard House is on the right.

Parking: Park in The Wayside lot on Hawthorne Lane, across from The Wayside.

Directions by public transportation: From downtown Boston, take MBTA Green Line to North Station. Take the MBTA Commuter Rail train (Fitchburg line) and get off at Concord Center. Orchard House is 1.2 miles from the station.

More information: This property is owned by the Louisa May Alcott Memorial Association. Website: www.louisamayalcott.org Phone: 978-369-4118

OTIS HOUSE

Boston, Massachusetts

Year Built: 1796

What's Special: *Elegant mansion, only one remaining in this section of Boston; designed by architect Charles Bulfinch*

Otis House is an impressive brick mansion designed in the Federal style by Charles Bulfinch, the renowned architect who also designed the gold-domed State House still in use today. Otis House was built for Harrison Gray Otis and his family. Otis was a wealthy lawyer who also was elected as a congressman, United States senator, and mayor of Boston. In addition, he was one of the developers who built the nearby Beacon Hill neighborhood, a highly lucrative venture.

The Otis House tour begins with a helpful introductory slide show to set the context. Otis House was originally one of numerous townhouses of the affluent in Bowdoin Square, which was one of the best locations in Boston in the late eighteenth century. As is often the case, the neighborhood changed dramatically over the ensuing years. (The destruction of the entire West End—which included Bowdoin Square and by the twentieth century had become home to working-class European immigrants—thanks to "urban renewal" in the late 1950s is a cautionary tale of urban planning gone badly awry.)

You will proceed to view a remarkable townhouse replete with elegant rooms, very spacious and exquisitely designed. The entry hall features a graceful staircase and very high ceilings. The dining parlor is large so as to accommodate the extensive entertaining that was customary for the Otis

Elizabeth S. Levy Merrick

family. It is resplendent with golden turquoise molding and wallpaper in the Pompeii style, which reflected the discoveries then resulting from excavations at Pompeii. Miniature classical busts are placed over doorways, continuing the Italian theme. Upstairs, the drawing room sparkles with its chandelier, mirrored doors, and Chinese reverse paintings on glass (designed to reflect light). The elaborate pink ceiling moldings are the finishing touch in the drawing room.

Later in the history of the house, it was operated as a genteel boarding house. Some boarders were doctors at neighboring Massachusetts General Hospital. One bedroom in the house is furnished and interpreted as a room for rent in the 1850s, when four sisters ran this respectable boarding house. Its amenities include a fireplace adapted for coal, a washstand, and a round "sitz bath" (small tub to sit in for bathing), which was stored under the bed.

Today, Otis House serves as headquarters for Historic New England in addition to being a house museum. Otis House is rightfully popular with both tourists and local historic-house fans. It is an uncommonly beautiful mansion with a fascinating history. Its downtown Boston location makes it very convenient to visit. In other words, there is every reason to visit this exceptional property.

To Visit

Location: 141 Cambridge Street, Boston, MA 02114

Opening hours: Year-round, Wednesday–Sunday, 11:00 a.m.–5:00 p.m. Tours every half hour, last tour at 4:30 p.m. Closed most major holidays. Open July 4.

Admission fees: $10/adults, $9/seniors, $5/students. Free for Historic New England members and Boston residents.

Directions by car: Located in downtown Boston on Cambridge Street.

Parking: Limited metered parking on street; also nearby public parking garages. Easiest to access by public transportation.

Directions by public transportation: Short walk from MBTA Red Line Charles Street/MGH Station; Blue Line Bowdoin Station (closed weekends); Green Line

Government Center Station (currently closed for construction); Green Line North Station.

More information: This property is owned by Historic New England. Website: www.historicnewengland.org Phone: 617-994-5920

Elizabeth S. Levy Merrick

PAUL REVERE HOUSE

Boston, Massachusetts

Year Built: c. 1680

What's Special: *Oldest house in downtown Boston; home of famous patriot leader; restored to seventeenth-century appearance; mostly original structure*

This must be the most famous historic house in Boston. Tourists come in droves. However, don't let that stop you from seeing this iconic house. It is the oldest house in downtown Boston, built around 1680, which would be reason enough to visit. But this is the home of Paul Revere, who is perhaps the most prominent patriot in the American collective memory thanks in large part to the Longfellow poem memorializing the midnight ride (with some poetic liberty).

Revere bought this house in 1770, and he and his family lived here for many years. He sold it out of the family in 1800. The house is still standing and open to the public today thanks to a Revere descendent who purchased it in the early twentieth century to save it from the threat of possible demolition. The many changes that were made to the house over the years have largely been removed or modified in order to restore the house to its original appearance.

The house is located on a picturesque square in Boston's North End, which became an Italian neighborhood well after Revere's time. It is a classic-looking seventeenth-century house with diamond-paned windows, First Period overhangs, and other characteristic features. The interior is furnished similarly to how it would have been when Paul Revere lived here, and upstairs rooms include numerous possessions of the Revere family. The rooms are whitewashed, with dark beams visible. There is also a charming Colonial garden in the small courtyard area, where there are several items made by Paul Revere and Sons, including a large bell.

Most visits here will be short, since it is a self-guided tour and there are few rooms. That may work out well for many visitors since the Paul Revere House is on the Freedom Trail with so many other wonderful historic sites to visit. Also, the Pierce/Hichborn House is next door, and a combination ticket can be purchased. Roaming the surrounding North End streets is in itself an adventure that will yield an incredible choice of authentic Italian restaurants to fuel your sightseeing.

To Visit

Location: 19 North Square, Boston, MA 02113

Opening hours: April 15–October 31, daily, 9:30 a.m. to 5:15 p.m. November 1–April 14, daily, 9:30 a.m. to 4:15 p.m. Closed on Mondays in January, February, and March. Closed on Thanksgiving, Christmas Day, and New Year's Day.

Admission fees: $3.50 /adults, $3/ seniors and college students, $1/children (ages five to seventeen).

Type of tour: Self-guided.

Directions by car: This house is centrally located in the North End neighborhood of Boston. Public transportation is the easiest way to get here.

Parking: Street parking is very limited, and the area is typically congested. There are public parking lots in downtown Boston within walking distance.

Directions by public transportation: Take the MBTA Green Line to Government Center (currently closed for construction) or Haymarket Stations; Blue Line to Government Center or Aquarium Stations; Orange Line to State or Haymarket Stations. Note that the Paul Revere House is on the Freedom Trail, marked by a red line on the pavement.

More information: This property is owned by the Paul Revere Memorial Association. Website: www.paulreverehouse.org Phone: 617-523-2338

PIERCE HOUSE

Dorchester (Boston), Massachusetts

Year Built: 1683

What's Special: Rare seventeenth-century house still standing in Boston; opportunity to see architectural features from different time periods

The Pierce House is something of a curiosity shop for those interested in architecture. When you drive up, the side of the house shows a classic seventeenth-century profile that will remind you of houses in Salem and elsewhere. But when you come to the front, it is the symmetry of Georgian style that is visible.

When you enter the Pierce House, you will immediately realize that this is not a place where you will feel enveloped in any particular bygone era. Only one room is shown in a way that fully reflects its historical (Georgian) appearance. The house is currently used primarily for school programs to introduce children to colonial life and Revolutionary War history. Nothing remains of the original twenty-acre farm, and the house is now cheek-by-jowl with multifamily houses of a much more recent vintage.

Nonetheless, historic-house fans—particularly those keen on architecture and construction methods— will find the Pierce House of interest. It was the home of the Pierce family for ten generations and started as a farmhouse of what we would today term a middle-class family. Thus it provides insight into the moderately prosperous but hard-working citizenry. Also, members of the Pierce family played a role in the revolution.

Its biggest appeal lies in the original architectural features that remain and the evidence of the many changes to the building over time. The

Elizabeth S. Levy Merrick

house still has low ceilings, an original built-in china cabinet, and original doors. A lean-to added later fortuitously preserved an entire exterior wall of seventeenth-century clapboards. In the attic there is evidence of some of the construction methods characteristic of the original building and later additions. Along the way, incidentally, you may spot nostalgic twentieth-century items, such as early radios and old jam bottles, left over from the last generation of Pierces to inhabit the home before the family generously donated it. The tour was rather like wandering through Grandma's house— if her house was built in 1683, that is.

To Visit

Location: 24 Oakton Avenue, Dorchester, MA 02122

Opening hours: Typically open four days per year. Check the website for specific dates.

Type of tour: Guided.

Admission fees: $5/ adults, $4/ seniors, $2.50/students, free for Historic New England members and Boston residents.

Directions by car: From downtown Boston, take I-93 South to Granite Avenue exit heading toward Ashmont. Continue straight onto Adams Street. Oakton Avenue is the seventh street on the right. House is on the left.

Parking: There is street parking on Oakton Avenue.

Directions by public transportation: Take the MBTA Red Line toward Ashmont/Braintree, get off at Fields Corner Station. Take the #202 bus (North Quincy Station via Adams Street and Keystone Apartments). Get off at intersection of Adams and Helena and walk a block down Adams to Oakton Street, where Pierce House is on the left.

More information: This property is owned by Historic New England. Website: www.historicnewengland.org Phone: 617-288-6041

Elizabeth S. Levy Merrick

PIERCE/HICHBORN HOUSE

Boston, Massachusetts

Year Built: 1711

What's Special: *Uncommon eighteenth-century brick house in Boston; relatively undiscovered despite its location*

The Pierce/Hichborn House is located next door to the Paul Revere House (across a small courtyard) in Boston's North End. A combination admission ticket for the two houses is available. Yet, the Pierce/Hichborn House sees far fewer visitors and is a way to delve into the eighteenth century without a lot of company.

The house has a very narrow façade on the street side because its front is actually located on the brick-paved alley that runs perpendicular to the street. It is remarkably different in appearance from the neighboring Paul Revere House. Built about thirty years later, the Pierce/Hichborn House is a brick dwelling designed in Georgian style. Moses Pierce, for whom the house was originally built, was a glazier—which explains why the windows are relatively plentiful and large for a tradesman's home of this time period. There is also a good deal of decorative brickwork on the exterior. The house was later purchased by Paul Revere's cousin Nathaniel Hichborn. In the nineteenth century, its rooms were rented to multiple immigrant families.

Inside, the compact house is filled with colonial furnishings that are not original to the house. It has many interesting features, including a line painted all along the beams in one room, apparently as a unique decoration for the ceiling. The fireplaces still show painting inside of the hearth, which is unusual. The house is full of character, and although tourists may throng just outside, it is easy to immerse yourself in its colonial story.

Be aware that this house is not always available for tours at the same times that the Paul Revere House is open. Call ahead if you want to make sure to catch the Pierce-Hichborn House, which is well worth a visit.

To Visit

Location: 19 North Square, Boston, MA 02113 (this is the address for purchasing admission—same as at Paul Revere House)

Opening hours: Tour days and times for the Pierce/Hichborn House are variable. Call ahead. The Paul Revere House—where tickets are purchased for the Pierce/Hichborn House—is open daily, April 15–October 31, 9:30 a.m. to 5:15 p.m.; November 1–April 14, 9:30 a.m. to 4:15 p.m. Closed on Mondays in January, February, and March. Closed on Thanksgiving, Christmas Day, and New Year's Day.

Type of tour: Guided.

Admission fees: $2

Directions by car: The Pierce/Hichborn House is centrally located in Boston's North End neighborhood. Public transportation is the easiest way to visit this house.

Parking: Street parking is very limited, and the area is typically congested. There are public parking lots in downtown Boston within walking distance.

Directions by public transportation: MBTA Green Line to Government Center (currently closed for construction) or Haymarket Stations; Blue Line to Government Center (currently closed for construction) or Aquarium Stations; Orange Line to State or Haymarket Stations. House is a short walk from any of these stations.

More information: This property is owned by the Paul Revere Memorial Association. Website: www.paulreverehouse.org Phone: (617) 523-2338

QUINCY HOMESTEAD

Quincy, Massachusetts

Year Built: 1686 with eighteenth-century additions

What's Special: *Home of illustrious American family; beautifully restored and furnished; lovely grounds*

The Quincy Homestead is probably best known today as the childhood home of Dorothy Quincy, who married the famed John Hancock. It was also the crown jewel in the vast holdings of the Quincy family, one of the most distinguished early families of Massachusetts whose descendants include President John Quincy Adams.

This large, gracious, and beautifully furnished mansion incorporates both the original seventeenth-century structure and eighteenth-century additions that remade the house in Georgian style. The addition not only enlarged the house but also made it grander and more formal. Most of the furnishings are not original but are antiques similar to what the Quincys would have had.

One highlight of the house tour is the parlor with its eighteenth-century French wallpaper and 1750 spinet. If you are fortunate, your guide may play the spinet for you. The harpsichord-like sounds fill the lovely parlor, and you may momentarily forget which century you inhabit. The kitchen is also very evocative, with wide plank floors, a huge hearth, and many artifacts from an earlier time. A carved wooden blanket chest from 1680 is a special item in this room, located in the oldest part of the house.

The house is set in park-like grounds that enhance the experience of visiting. Adjacent to the house is a formal garden planted with boxwood

Elizabeth S. Levy Merrick

to reflect the original garden plan. There is also an herb garden with plants appropriate to a colonial-era kitchen garden.

Many generations of the Quincy family lived here until a reversal of fortune due to failed investments led to the estate being auctioned off. In the early 1900s, the Colonial Dames of America took it over as a house museum in partnership with the Commonwealth of Massachusetts. The Colonial Dames continue to show it to the public. This remarkable historic house is a delight.

To Visit

Location: 34 Butler Road, Quincy, MA 02169

Opening hours: May–September, one Saturday per month. Check the website in the spring for specific dates. Tours start at 1:00 p.m. and occur every half-hour with the last one at 3:30 p.m.

Type of tour: Guided.

Admission fees: Free, but voluntary donation suggested.

Directions by car: From Boston, take the Southeast Expressway (Routes 3 and 93) to exit 8, Furnace Brook Parkway. Continue on the Parkway for exactly two miles. Turn right onto Hancock Street. Take the first left onto Butler Road. The Quincy Homestead is on immediate left.

Parking: Street parking is available.

Directions by public transportation: From Boston, take the MBTA Red Line toward Braintree, to Quincy Center Station. At the bus station there, take the #210 bus toward North Quincy Station via Hancock Street. Get off at Hancock Street and Butler Road. Walk down Butler Road just a few minutes to the Quincy Homestead.

More information: This property is owned by the Colonial Dames of America. Website: www.nscda.org Phone: 617-742-3190

Elizabeth S. Levy Merrick

QUINCY HOUSE

Quincy, Massachusetts

Year Built: 1770

What's Special: *Home of noteworthy family in early America; Revolutionary War connections; furnished in Victorian style; unusual "monitor roof"*

This large Georgian house was built as a country home for Colonel Josiah Quincy and remained in the Quincy family for several generations. Originally part of a 250-acre estate stretching to Quincy Bay, only the impressive house and a small parcel of land remain. From the spacious center hall to light-filled rooms, however, the house still exudes an aura of country ease. In the summer, ocean breezes waft through the house, which is just a short distance from the coast. A small but evocative flower garden adds charm to the modest lawn currently surrounding the house.

"Country" does not mean "rustic" in this house, as the graceful columned portico immediately shows. Wealth and good taste are reflected in elegance throughout. Many of the furnishings are from the Quincy family. A recent interior restoration has turned the clock to the late nineteenth century when Eliza Susan Quincy, a descendent who carefully recorded her family's history, lived there. The reproduction canvas floor covering in the entry hall, stenciled with richly colored geometrics, reflects this period.

All three floors are open to visitors. The top floor is actually the interior of the monitor roof: a half-story enclosure with windows on all sides. This is the oldest example of this type of roof to survive from colonial days. It was through these monitor roof windows that Colonel Quincy witnessed the momentous departure of the British during the evacuation of Boston in 1775. He etched words to this effect in a roof window pane, which was later removed and framed and is now on display. Visitors can also view servants' quarters on the third floor.

The Quincy family story reflects that of many families in the colonies in the revolutionary period. One son, Josiah, was a patriot like his father; another was a loyalist who left during the revolution and never returned. The younger Josiah joined with John Adams in the controversial act of serving as defense attorneys for the British accused in the Boston Massacre, in the interest of the rule of law. Colonel Quincy was well-connected with prominent figures of the period, including George Washington, John Adams, and Benjamin Franklin. Franklin reportedly dined with the family during the Siege of Boston in 1775 and stayed overnight in what henceforth was known as the Franklin bedroom.

The Quincys remained prominent in later generations. Colonel Quincy's grandson, Josiah Quincy III, became the second mayor of Boston and entertained extensively at the house. Later on, several unmarried female members of the family remained in the home, preserving both the house and the stories associated with it. The house was sold out of the family in 1895 by the last Quincy daughter's heir, but other relations later repurchased the house and donated it as a house museum. This was fortunate for posterity, since the history-filled Quincy House is now open for the general public to experience.

To Visit

Location: 20 Muirhead Street, Quincy, MA 02170

Opening hours: June–October, first Saturday of the month, 1:00–5:00 p.m. Tours on the hour. Last tour at 4:00 p.m.

Admission fees: $5/adults, $4/seniors, $2.50/students, free for Historic New England members and Quincy residents.

Type of tour: Guided.

Directions by car: From Boston, take I-93 South and get off at exit 12 (Gallivan Boulevard). Follow signs for Quincy Shore Drive, and stay on it for 1.9 miles. Turn right onto West Elm Avenue, then right onto Staunton Street—stay on as it curves to right. Take the first left onto Muirhead Street.

Parking: There is plenty of street parking.

Directions by public transportation: Take the MBTA Red Line to Wollaston Station. Turn left on Beale Street, walk about half a mile (Beale Street turns into Beach Street after crossing Hancock Street) to Muirhead Street, and turn right. House will be on your left.

More information: This property is owned by Historic New England. Website: www.historicnewengland.org Phone: 617-994-5930

RALPH WALDO EMERSON HOUSE

Concord, Massachusetts

Year Built: 1828

What's Special: Longtime home of Ralph Waldo Emerson; substantial eighteenth-century house; mostly original furnishings

This lovely house was home to celebrated Transcendentalist philosopher and poet Ralph Waldo Emerson and his family over several decades. It was a hub of intellectual life during Emerson's day. The Ralph Waldo Emerson House is still in the family, owned by an association including Emerson descendants. Its stellar namesake notwithstanding, it somehow maintains the comfortable feel of a family residence even though no one has lived there since 1930.

Emerson and his second wife, Lidian, moved into the house in 1835. Emerson wrote many of his important works here and lived in the house until his death in 1882. The house is high-ceilinged and elegant, with a center hall. The furnishings are largely original and include personal belongings, such as Emerson's silk academic robe. In the nursery, there are toys that belonged to Emerson's children.

There are numerous rooms with great charm, including the spacious bedroom with bay windows and original four-poster bed. The parlor sometimes was the meeting place of the Transcendental Club (not always referred to as such during Emerson's lifetime), a discussion group for liberal-minded thinkers in a variety of professions. Emerson's study is the only one in the house with reproduction furnishings; the originals were moved long ago to the Concord Museum. The house has on display

Elizabeth S. Levy Merrick

portraits and photographs of Emerson family members as well as illustrious friends and acquaintances.

Tours are conducted on a continual basis. When you arrive, you join the one in progress, and then continue on to the next tour to catch the earlier part you may have missed. Although you will not have to spend time waiting for a tour, you should be sure to visit the pleasant garden in back. Note that there is a path that leads to Walden Pond and surrounding woods, made most famous by Emerson's fellow Transcendantalist Henry David Thoreau. Ask for directions so you can enjoy more time in this archetypal New England landscape.

To Visit

Location: 28 Cambridge Turnpike, Concord, MA 01742

Directions by car: From Boston, take Storrow Drive, continuing on Soldiers Field Road to Eliot Bridge, following signs for MA-2/US-3/Arlington/Fresh Pond Parkway. Follow Fresh Pond Parkway and Alewife Brook Parkway to intersection with Route 2. Make a left onto Route 2 West. Where Route 2 takes a sharp left, stay straight and continue onto Cambridge Turnpike. The Ralph Waldo Emerson House is on this road.

Parking: On-street parking available.

Directions by public transportation: From Boston, take the MBTA Green Line to North Station. At North Station, take the MBTA commuter rail Fitchburg/South Acton Line-Fitchburg, and get off at Concord Station. Ralph Waldo Emerson House is about a twenty-minute walk from the station.

Opening hours: Late April–October. Thursday–Saturday, 10:00 a.m.–4:30 p.m., and Sunday 1:00–4:30 p.m. Monday holidays 1:00–4:30 p.m.

Fees: $9/adults, $7/seniors and students seven to seventeen. Children under seven free.

More information: This property is owned by the Ralph Waldo Emerson Memorial Association. Website: www.facebook.com/EmersonHouseConcord Phone: 978-369-2236.

Elizabeth S. Levy Merrick

ROYALL HOUSE AND SLAVE QUARTERS

Medford, Massachusetts

Year Built: 1732–1737 (incorporating seventeenth-century structure)

What's Special: Beautifully preserved Georgian mansion; original free-standing slave quarters; Revolutionary War connections; focus on interpretation of lives of both wealthy owners and enslaved people; park setting

A visitor to the Royall House in 1750 called it "one of the grandest houses in North America." This Georgian mansion still conveys the elegance than impressed that long-ago visitor. It is located on a small but pretty remnant of the vast estate it once crowned, in the densely built neighborhood that grew up around it long after the loyalist Royall family fled the American Revolution.

The house incorporates a seventeenth-century farmhouse, built on the six hundred–acre Ten Hills Farm land grant to Governor John Winthrop. Its current appearance reflects extensive additions and remodeling by the Royall family in the eighteenth century. Isaac Royall Sr. and his family moved there in 1737, along with 27 enslaved Africans. He owned a Caribbean cane plantation and dealt in rum, sugar, and slaves. Isaac Royall Jr. inherited the house in 1739. He made further changes and maintained the family's status and wealth.

The Royall House and Slave Quarters offers a look at the intertwined lives of these wealthy loyalists and the enslaved Africans who served them. The Royalls were the largest slave-holders in Massachusetts. Close to the house is the only free-standing slave quarters remaining in the northern United States. Although the interior was converted years ago to a meeting and exhibit space, this physical artifact of Northern slavery provides a focal point for considering the very different lives of slaves and masters. It houses an archaeological exhibit that sheds light on some generally unrecorded aspects of life under slavery. It also hosts interesting lectures and other events throughout the year, often related to the history of slavery. Of note, one of the Africans enslaved at the Royall House property, Belinda, played a significant role in this history. In her old age, as a formerly enslaved person, she successfully petitioned the Massachusetts legislature after the revolution for a pension from the Royall estate in light of her years of uncompensated labor.

The mansion has two lovely facades, one including Palladian windows and wood surfaces carved to resemble stone blocks. One remaining side of an octagonal summerhouse reminds us of the refined gazebo-like structure that previously sat amid formal gardens. Inside, the mahogany banister gracing the main stairway, large windows, Delft-tiled fireplaces, and carved paneling reflect luxurious design. There are period furnishings and artifacts; only a handful belonged to the Royalls. The tour also highlights utilitarian rooms occupied by enslaved Africans working to run the household.

The property has numerous Revolutionary War connections. Isaac Royall Jr. left at the outset of the revolution. Paul Revere's midnight ride brought him past the house. The house became military headquarters for General John Stark and others. George Washington came to the Royall House to meet with them and reportedly interrogated two British deserters there.

The Royall House and Slave Quarters is a unique house museum that is a window into the lives of both wealthy white colonials and enslaved people in the North—a complex American story that deserves to be told.

To Visit

Location: 15 George Street, Medford, MA 02155

Opening hours: Mid-May–late October, Saturday and Sunday. Tours at 1:00, 2:00, and 3:00 p.m.

Elizabeth S. Levy Merrick

Type of tour: Guided tour of mansion; self-guided tour of slave quarters and exhibits.

Admission fees: To view the mansion, $7/adults, $5/seniors and students, $4/children seventeen and younger, $16/family rate (up to two adults, up to four children under eighteen). Admission to slave quarters is free. Free for active-duty military personnel and their families from Memorial Day through Labor Day, and for Royall House Association members.

Directions by car: From Boston, take I-93 North to exit 32. Proceed west on Route 60 (Salem Street), following signs toward Medford Square to second light. Bear left to enter Main Street going south. Bear right at Mobil Station to stay on Main Street and proceed to intersection of Main Street and George Street. Make a right on George Street, proceed one half block, and park on the right.

Parking: Street parking available.

Directions by public transportation: MBTA Buses #96 from MBTA Red Line Stations at Harvard Square or Davis Square and #101 from MBTA Orange Line Station at Sullivan Square stop at the Royall House as they proceed to and from Medford Square.

More information: This museum is owned by the Royall House Association. Website: www.royallhouse.org Phone: 781-396-9032

SHIRLEY-EUSTIS HOUSE

Roxbury (Boston), Massachusetts

Year Built: 1747

What's Special: *Country residence of two Massachusetts governors; impressive Georgian mansion with Federal modifications; Revolutionary war connections; beautiful gardens and orchard*

The Shirley-Eustis House, or Shirley Place, is an inner-city hidden gem that richly rewards its relatively small number of visitors. When you catch your first glimpse of this magnificent mansion, restored to its Federal-era appearance and set within an acre of bucolic gardens, you will be amazed. It is a beautiful gift from the past that has survived as the modern city engulfed everything around it. This neighborhood sees few tourists, but the house is easy to access by public transportation, car, or taxi.

This house was built to impress, and it still does. As the country residence of Royal Governor William Shirley, who had it built, and of the nineteenth-century governor William Eustis, it saw many important visitors and social events. The spaciousness of the mansion and its exquisite architectural features convey both beauty and grandeur. The façade has white pilasters (flattened columns) stretching to the roof line. A large cupola adds to the imposing appearance.

The building has been restored to its Federal-era appearance around 1800. The two-story great hall, where dinners and balls were held, has a curved musicians' gallery. There is also a large door with a Palladian window above and intricately carved Corinthian pilasters surrounding it, which led to gardens that no longer exist. The great hall was the site of a reception for Revolutionary War hero the Marquis de Lafayette. Governor Shirley and his wife still preside in the hall, at least in portraits.

A graceful floating staircase invites a trip to the second floor. Upstairs, there are some furnished rooms and others given over to exhibits on architectural changes over time, personal effects of Governor Eustis, and maps showing the area at different time periods. High ceilings create an airy feeling, and large windows let light pour into every room. Few of the furnishings are original to the house, but they are antiques representing various time periods and styles.

The restoration of the building is a story unto itself. By the late nineteenth century, the house had fallen on hard times. It was turned into tenement housing. By 1911 the deteriorated structure was abandoned. Early preservationists saved it, but it was not until 1991 that it was restored and opened to the public. Photos document the restoration process.

Stop in to the Carriage House (moved from elsewhere but similar to the original) and stroll out to the gazebo (also not original to the property but lovely). The gardens contain flowers popular at the time the house was built. The apple orchard has some original trees and includes Roxbury Russets, an heirloom apple prized by connoisseurs. This peaceful setting must have been more tumultuous when, during the revolution, the famous cannons from Fort Ticonderoga passed by the house—those same cannons that convinced the British to finally evacuate Boston.

To Visit

Location: 33 Shirley Street, Roxbury, MA 02119

Opening hours: Memorial Day–Labor Day, Thursday–Sunday, 1:00–4:00 p.m. Tours on the hour (last tour at 3:00 p.m.). Labor Day–Columbus Day, weekends only. Appointments can be made year-round.

Type of tour: Guided.

Admission fees: $5/ adults, $4/seniors and students.

Directions by car: From downtown Boston, take Massachusetts Avenue South past Boston Medical Center, and continue one half mile to Shirley Street on the right, just before the railroad overpass. Turn right onto Shirley Street and proceed four blocks. The house is on the left at the top of the hill. Or you can take I-93 South to exit 18 for Massachusetts Avenue/Roxbury. Turn left at the stoplight at Massachusetts Avenue and proceed one half mile to Shirley Street on the right, just before the railroad overpass. Turn right onto Shirley Street and proceed four blocks. The house is on the left at the top of the hill.

Parking: There is plenty of street parking.

Directions by public transportation: Take the MBTA Orange Line to Ruggles Station, then catch bus #15 to Dudley Square and Shirley Street.

More information: This property is owned by the Shirley-Eustis House Association. Website: www.shirleyeustishouse.org Phone: 617-442-2275

Directions by public transportation: From downtown Boston, take the MBTA Red Line toward Ashmont, and get off at Andrew Square Station. Walk from Andrew Square Station (note, part of the route is somewhat industrial) or take the #17 Fields Corner via Kane Square bus, getting off on Boston Street at Harvest Street.

More information: This property is owned by the Dorchester Historical Society. Website: www.dorchesterhistoricalsociety.org Phone: (617) 293-3052

Elizabeth S. Levy Merrick

WILLIAM HICKLING PRESCOTT HOUSE

Boston, Massachusetts

Year Built: 1808

What's special: *Elegant Federal townhouse; overlay of grand Victorian style; spectacular Back Bay location*

The William Hickling Prescott House consists of two adjoining brick townhouses built in the Federal style by renowned architect Asher Benjamin. The Prescott House reflects the height of sophistication, with bow-front facades, columns, and pilasters throughout. It is named after one of its owners, William Hickling Prescott, who was among the first American-born historians. His well-respected scholarship (focused mainly on Spanish history) is especially remarkable given that he was blinded in a freak accident at a young age, as part of a food fight for which Harvard students of the era were notorious.

Prescott House is situated at the edge of Boston Common, affording splendid views of what is now iconic green space. When the house was built, however, it had a harbor view. It was only later that this section of waterfront was filled in to form the Back Bay neighborhood, now one of the most desirable in the city. Interestingly, the land was previously owned by American portraitist John Singleton Copley.

Rooms are beautifully furnished in a variety of periods spanning the eighteenth and nineteenth centuries, although few furnishings are original. Highlights of this large and lovely residence include William Prescott's study in a later addition to the house. The study is restored to its original appearance and complete with a secret staircase down to the library. There is a Victorian-era grand staircase. On the second (of five) floors, the sparkling ballroom beckons with windows reaching from the floor to the very high ceiling, decorated in Victorian style.

Currently the house is also the headquarters of the Massachusetts chapter of the Society of Colonial Dames of America. There are mannequins dressed in period costumes in several spots in the house, adding another note of interest.

The location of Prescott House makes it easy to combine a visit here with touring other historic houses in Back Bay and Beacon Hill (including Gibson House and Nichols House). And with quaint, bustling Charles Street just a few minutes' walk from here, interesting dining and shopping await as well.

To Visit

Location: 55 Beacon St., Boston, MA 02108

Opening hours: June–August, Wednesday, Thursday, and Saturday, 12:00–4:00 p.m. Tours at 12:15, 1:30, and 2:45 p.m. In September, Thursday and Saturday only, same hours.

Type of tour: Guided.

Admission fees: $7. Free for active military members and their families.

Directions by car: House is in downtown Boston, in the Back Bay section of the city. Beacon Street is a main thoroughfare. It is easiest to visit this house by public transportation.

Parking: There is street parking in the area, but it can be very difficult to find available spots. There is a parking garage underneath Boston Common, and other parking garages are in the area.

Directions by public transportation: Take the MBTA Red Line to Park Street Station, and then walk through Boston Common to Beacon Street. Equally convenient is to take the MBTA Green Line to Arlington Station. Walk up

Arlington Street along the edge of Boston Common, and go right onto Beacon Street. The house is a ten-minute walk from either of these T stations.

More information: This property is owned by the National Society of Colonial Dames of America. Website: www.nscda.org Phone: 617-742-3190